T0167681

Currency Unions

Currency Unions

EDITED BY

Alberto Alesina and
Robert J. Barro

HOOVER INSTITUTION PRESS
Stanford University
Stanford, California

Hoover Institution Press Publication No. 496
Copyright © 2001 by the Board of Trustees of the
   Leland Stanford Junior University

First printing 2001
06   05   04   03   02   01   9   8   7   6   5   4   3   2   1

Manufactured in the United States of America
The paper used in this publication meets the minimum requirements
of American National Standard for Information Sciences—Permanence
of Paper for Printed Library Materials, ANSI Z39.48–1984. ♾

Library of Congress Cataloging-in-Publication Data
Currency unions / edited by Alberto Alesina and Robert J. Barro.
        p.   cm.
   Based on a conference held at the Hoover Institution in May 2000.
"The present volume includes non-technical summaries of these papers . . ." [Introduction]
   Includes bibliographical references and index.
   ISBN 0-8179-2842-1 (alk. paper)
   1. Monetary unions—Congresses.   2. Monetary policy—International cooperation—Congresses.
3. Currency question—Congresses.   4. Debts, External—Congresses.   5. Financial crises—Congresses.
6. International trade—Congresses.   7. International finance—Congresses.   8. International Monetary
Fund—Congresses.   I. Alesina, Alberto.   II. Barro, Robert J.
HG3894 .C87   2001
332.4'566—dc21   2001039204

Contents

Acknowledgments

This volume on currency unions had its origins in the conference that we held at the Hoover Institution, Stanford University, in May 2000. Hoover provided a great environment for the conference, and we are indebted to Director John Raisian for providing this attractive venue. We also owe to John the funding that enabled us to assemble the outstanding group of scholars who participated in the meeting. Hoover associate director Richard Sousa functioned essentially as a co-organizer of the conference, and we deeply appreciate his input and assistance. In addition, we would like to acknowledge the outstanding organizational skills of Teresa Judd and Deborah Ventura.

About the Authors

Alberto Alesina received his Ph.D. in 1986 from Harvard, where he became full professor in 1993. He has written two books and many research papers in the area of economic policy and political economy which have been published in leading academic journals. He is an editor of the *Quarterly Journal of Economics*.

Robert J. Barro is Robert C. Waggoner Professor of Economics at Harvard University, a senior fellow at the Hoover Institution at Stanford University and a columnist for *Business Week*. He has written extensively on macroeconomic topics. Recent research has focused on the determinants of economic growth and the role of dollarization. Recent books include *Determinants of Economic Growth* and *Getting It Right: Markets and Choices in a Free Society*, both from MIT Press.

Eduardo Borensztein is the chief of the Developing Countries Studies Division of the Research Department of the International Monetary Fund, where he has also worked in the Asian and African departments. He received his Ph.D. in economics from the Massachusetts

Institute of Technology (MIT) and an undergraduate degree from the Universidad de Buenos Aires. He has also worked at the Central Bank of Argentina and at FIEL, a private research institute in Buenos Aires. He has published extensively in the areas of comparisons of exchange rate systems, currency crises, financial and foreign exchange markets, and transition economies.

Christian Broda is a Ph.D. student of economics at MIT. His current research looks at the effects of uncertainty under different exchange rate regimes. He also has written about dollarization, optimal regulation in banking sectors with two currencies, and the lender-of-last-resort function of central banks. He was educated at the Universidad de San Andrés in Buenos Aires, Argentina.

Guillermo Calvo is director of the Center for International Economics and Distinguished University Professor, University of Maryland, and will become the chief economist at the Inter-American Development Bank. He was professor of economics at Columbia University and the University of Pennsylvania and senior adviser at the International Monetary Fund. His current research focuses on capital flow volatility and international financial architecture.

Luis Felipe Céspedes is a Ph.D. student at New York University (NYU). Previously, he worked as an economist at the Macroeconomic Advisory Group of Chile's Finance Ministry. His main areas of interest are international finance, macroeconomics, and monetary policy. He will be joining the Research Department at the International Monetary Fund.

Roberto Chang is an associate professor of economics at Rutgers University, New Brunswick, New Jersey. Previously, he was a research officer at the Federal Reserve Bank of Atlanta and an assistant professor at NYU. Professor Chang has published extensively on international economics and macroeconomic policy. His current work focuses on financial fragility in emerging markets, exchange rate regimes, and dollarization.

Charles Engel is professor of economics and public affairs at the University of Wisconsin and research associate at the National Bureau of Economic Research. He has held previous appointments at the University of Virginia and the University of Washington. He received his Ph.D. from the University of California. His research is in international macroeconomics.

Stanley Fischer is the first deputy managing director of the International Monetary Fund. Prior to taking up his position at the Fund in 1994, Mr. Fischer was the Killian Professor and the head of the Department of Economics at MIT. He took the B.Sc. (Economics) and M.Sc. (Economics) at the London School of Economics from 1962 to 1966 and obtained his Ph.D. in economics at MIT in 1969. Mr. Fischer is the author of *Macroeconomics* (with Rudi Dornbusch) and of several other books. He has published extensively in professional journals.

Jeffrey Frankel is Harpel Chair at Harvard University's Kennedy School of Government and directs the National Bureau of Economic Research program in International Finance and Macroeconomics. He served as a member of President Clinton's Council of Economic Advisers (1996–99), with responsibility for international economics, macroeconomics, and the environment. Before that, he was professor of economics at the University of California, Berkeley. He has had appointments at the Institute for International Economics, International Monetary Fund, Federal Reserve Board, Brookings Institution, University of Michigan, Yale University, and the World Bank. His Ph.D. is from M.I.T.

Maurice Obstfeld is the Class of 1958 Professor of Economics at the University of California, Berkeley. His interests are in international finance and macroeconomics, areas in which he has published a number of research articles. Professor Obstfeld received his Ph.D. from MIT, later teaching at Columbia, the University of Pennsylvania, and Harvard before moving to Berkeley. He has served as a consultant for the IMF, World Bank, European Commission, and several central banks. He is a research associate of the National Bureau of Economic Research, a research fellow of the Centre for Economic Policy Research, and a fellow of the Econometric Society.

Carmen M. Reinhart is a professor at the Department of Economics and the School of Public Affairs at the University of Maryland. She is the director of the International Security and Economic Policy Specialization at the School of Public Affairs and a research associate at the National Bureau of Economic Research. She serves on several editorial boards, including those of the *American Economic Review* and the *Journal of International Economics*. She writes on a variety of topics in international finance, including international capital flows, financial crises, and exchange rate programs.

Kenneth Rogoff is a professor of economics at Harvard University. He has formerly held staff positions at the Board of Governors of the Federal Reserve Board and the International Monetary Fund. In 1986, he was a national fellow at the Hoover Institution.

Andrew K. Rose is the Bernard T. Rocca Jr. Professor of International Trade at Haas School of Business at the University of California, Berkeley. His current research has focused on international trade patterns, contagion in currency crises, exchange rate determination, banking and exchange crises in developing countries, and exchange rate regimes. He is the managing editor of the *Journal of International Economics*, a research associate at the National Bureau of Economic Research, and a research fellow of the Center for Economic Policy Research. Rose holds a Ph.D. in economics from MIT and an M.A. in philosophy from the University of Oxford.

Andrés Velasco is Sumitomo-FASID Professor of Finance and Development at the Kennedy School of Government at Harvard University. He has published widely in the areas of international economics, economic development, and political economy. His current research focuses on the causes of financial crises in emerging markets and identifying policies that can help avoid such crises. Velasco holds a Ph.D. in economics from Columbia University and M.A. and B.A. degrees from Yale University. He is affiliated with the National Bureau of Economic Research in Cambridge and the Center for Applied Economics at the University of Chile.

Jeromin Zettelmeyer is an economist in the Developing Country Studies Division of the International Monetary Fund's Research Department. He has also worked in the IMF's European II department. He has a Ph.D. from MIT and an economics degree from the University of Bonn. His publications and research interests are in the areas of monetary policy, exchange rate regimes, international financial architecture, and macroeconomic aspects of transition.

Alberto Alesina
Robert J. Barro

Introduction

During the post–World War II period, the number of independent countries more than doubled, to nearly two hundred today. Until recently, most countries had their own currencies. Hence, the expansion of the number of countries led to a proliferation of the number of currencies. More recently, however, the identification of currencies with countries has weakened, and the discussion has shifted toward one of desirable forms and sizes of currency unions.

The growing policy significance of currency unions motivated us to organize a conference at the Hoover Institution in May 2000. We brought together about two dozen economists who were experts on international monetary topics. The idea was to consider basic conceptual issues about currency unions and other monetary regimes, including flexible and fixed exchange rates. We sought also to assess the available empirical evidence on the performance of these alternative monetary systems. Finally, we hoped to reach some policy conclusions, notably on the desirability of currency unions for countries in various circumstances.

The conference included eight academic papers, many of which will likely appear in a special issue of Harvard University's *Quarterly Journal of Economics*. The present volume includes nontechnical summaries of these papers, along with the text of a dinner address that was presented at the conference by Stan Fischer, the first deputy managing director of the International Monetary Fund.

Individual currencies are sometimes valued out of national pride, although one would have expected these feelings to be more intense for language than for money. Yet many countries willingly use the language of another country, typically the one of a former colonial ruler. Given this acceptance of transplanted language, it is surprising how often people reject currency unions—which sometimes involve the use of another country's currency—simply on the grounds that important countries are supposed to have their own money.

From an economic standpoint, the strongest argument for individual money is that it allows a country to pursue its own monetary policy. In theory, if the country operates with a flexible exchange rate, the monetary authority can design a policy that responds optimally to its own economic disturbances. Typically, the desired policy will look *countercyclical*, that is, expansionary during recessions and contractionary in booms. In contrast, under a fixed exchange rate, monetary policy has to be subordinated to the maintenance of the exchange rate. Fixed exchange rate regimes include a peg to another currency—which may or may not be permanent—as well as the more serious commitment represented by a currency board or dollarization (by which we mean one country's use of another country's money).

Luis Céspedes, Roberto Chang, and Andrés Velasco make the traditional case for flexible exchange rates and countercyclical monetary policy in a modern theoretical framework that includes a detailed analysis of a country's financial structure. They argue that an independent monetary policy and a flexible exchange rate can be useful even for developing countries that have substantial foreign currency debt. Maurice Obstfeld and Kenneth Rogoff also look at the workings of monetary policy under flexible exchange rates. They argue that this type of policy can work out well even if central banks determine their actions independently, rather than coordinating with the banks of other countries.

However, as Guillermo Calvo and Carmen Reinhart argue in their paper, many central banks in supposedly flexible exchange rate systems have been unable in practice to carry out policies that look desirable, much less optimal. Empirically, the typical monetary authority has a "fear of floating" and, therefore, does not allow the exchange rate to move in a way that would permit a countercyclical monetary policy.

Two other papers in this volume reach somewhat different conclusions. Christian Broda argues empirically that countries that operate under flexible exchange rates have performed better than fixed rate countries in their responses to terms-of-trade shocks. Presumably, the better performance results from the extra freedom for monetary policy in the floating rate systems. Eduardo Borensztein and Jeromin Zettelmeyer carried out case studies for several countries and found that all monetary authorities are, to some extent, dependent on the interest rate policy set by the U.S. Federal Reserve. However, this dependence is much less for flexible rate countries than for those that commit to a fixed exchange rate by operating a currency board.

In our paper for this volume, we extend Robert Mundell's classic and Nobel Prize–winning analysis of optimum currency areas to bring together the various elements that determine the optimal sizes of currency unions. We allow for a possible benefit from independent monetary policy, but we also argue that dollarization conveys a valuable commitment to price stability (assuming that the anchor currency, which could be the U.S. dollar or the euro, is properly managed). Under dollarization, sound monetary and exchange rate policies no longer depend on the intelligence and discipline of domestic policymakers. Their monetary policy becomes essentially the one followed by the anchor country (which could be the United States), and the exchange rate is fixed forever.

Our analysis also incorporates the benefits of a common currency in stimulating international commerce in goods and services and in financial transactions. The expansion of world trade—or globalization—has made it increasingly inconvenient for each country to use its own money. This factor and two others seem to explain why the world has been moving away from the doctrine of one country, one currency and toward multicountry currency unions. The first additional factor is the already noted dramatic increase in the number of independent countries. For the many small, independent countries that have been created since the end of World War II, the costs in terms of forgone trade of maintaining one's own currency are particularly high. The second additional consideration is that the benefit that economists and central bankers attribute to independent monetary policy has diminished as we all have learned to value price stability over active macroeconomic stabilization. In the 1960s and 1970s, there was much greater confidence that monetary expansion and inflation—either in general or in the form of countercyclical policy—would convey benefits in terms of higher economic growth and lower unemployment. Now there is widespread belief that monetary authorities should concentrate on providing a stable nominal framework and otherwise staying out of the way.

Roughly sixty small countries or territories have for some time been members of currency unions or have used a large country's money. Examples are the fifteen-member CFA franc zone in Africa, the seven-member Eastern Caribbean Currency Area, the use of the U.S. dollar by Panama and several smaller countries, the use of the Belgian franc by Luxembourg and the Swiss franc by Liechtenstein, and the use of the Israeli shekel in the West Bank and Gaza.

Andrew Rose has been studying the economic performance of these existing currency unions, and the present volume summarizes his joint papers presented at the conference—one with Charles Engel and another with Jeffrey Frankel. One major finding is that a currency union dramatically expands the volume of international trade among the members, by something like a factor of three. Moreover, heightened international trade contributes to higher long-run economic growth. Members of currency unions seem also to maintain more correlated movements of prices and outputs. However, there was not much evidence that the currency union countries carried out superior macroeconomic policies, except for the avoidance of extreme inflation.

The Rose program of empirical research on existing currency unions has sometimes been criticized for focusing on small and therefore nonrepresentative economies. Of course, this focus is dictated by the available data—in the future, when currency unions will likely be more plentiful among larger countries, the data will be much better. However, even at present, one can regard the existing unions as providing interesting experiments about the effects of alternative monetary systems. Consider, as a contrast, the plight of researchers on school choice, who eagerly examine the data for a few thousand students who are the subject of short-lived experimental programs. In the case of the small currency union economies, we are effectively receiving experimental data for hundreds of thousands of people who have submitted themselves to an economic experiment about the role of the monetary system.

The notion that currency unions will be more prevalent among large countries in the future is supported by the recently formed union of the twelve European countries that use the euro. Several other countries may sign on later—although Denmark said no, and the debate in the United Kingdom is intense. Dollarization has been contemplated by several countries in Latin America, including Argentina, Peru, and much of Central America. Argentina went part of the way toward dollarization through its adoption of a currency board linked to the U.S. dollar in 1991. Currency boards that lock local currencies to the dollar or the euro also exist in Hong Kong, Estonia, Bulgaria, and Lithuania. In November 2000, El Salvador announced its determination fully to dollarize, and, as a positive sign of the times, this decision received immediate support from the U.S. Treasury and the International Monetary Fund.

From a scientific standpoint, an exciting development is the dollarization in Ecuador. The history of this decision and an analysis of its likely consequences are provided in Stan Fischer's paper from the conference. Ecuador had experienced severe economic and political problems for some time, but the situation appeared to brighten in 1998 with the election as president of Jamil Mahuad, who had been a successful reformer as mayor of Quito. However, he was unable to gather the political support needed to solve problems of the public finances, subsidies on consumer goods, foreign debt, and the banking sector. When bank runs occurred in March 1999, he responded by freezing deposits. This action was extremely controversial and resulted in an arrest warrant after Mahuad was forced to move to the United States.

Mahuad proposed dollarization in Ecuador in early January 2000 not as part of a coherent economic plan but because he became desperate to do something dramatic when his approval rating fell below 10 percent. Although the proposal led to a rise in his popularity rating, it was not enough to save Mahuad's presidency, and he was soon ousted in a bloodless coup. However, his vice president and successor, Gustavo Noboa, recognized the potential effectiveness and popularity of dollarization and, therefore, moved aggressively to make the U.S. dollar the currency of Ecuador. The transition was nearly complete by September 2000. No doubt, the process of obtaining the U.S. dollars needed to replace the Ecuadorian sucres was aided by the high price of oil, Ecuador's main export.

There is an ongoing debate over whether major monetary reforms, such as dollarization, can be successful without preconditions, especially sound fiscal and banking practices. Ecuador is, therefore, interesting because none of these preconditions existed. In fact, these deficiencies were part of the crisis atmosphere, and the crisis generated the political consensus to do something drastic, namely, dollarization. In other words, the lack of supposed preconditions explains why dollarization occurred in Ecuador. (In contrast, El Salvador is in much better shape in overall economic policy, and the recently announced dollarization had been contemplated for many years.) The crucial question for Ecuador is whether, once in place, dollarization will help to cure other problems, such as fiscal imbalances and banking inadequacies, so that the missing preconditions become fulfilled postconditions.

One temporary problem in Ecuador—caused by the sharpness of the currency devaluation in 1999—is that inflation for 2000 was very high. This behavior reflects a onetime adjustment toward "purchasing power parity." That is, the dollar prices of goods and services in Ecuador became very low in 1999 because the currency devaluation was proportionately much greater than the rise in the domestic (sucre) price level. With the dollarization in place, Ecuador's inflation should recede.

Aside from the temporary inflation, dollarization seems to be serving in Ecuador as a foundation for the resolution of other economic problems. Progress has been made with international debtors, and some domestic reforms have been accomplished. Of course, it is too early to tell whether this grand experiment by a small, poor country will prove to be successful. One thing for sure is that we will learn not only from Ecuador but also from the move toward currency unions throughout the world.

Stanley Fischer

1
Ecuador and the International Monetary Fund

Ecuador's decision to dollarize was taken in January 2000 by then President Jamil Mahuad, who only a few days before had described the idea as "a jump into the abyss." So it seemed. But although President Mahuad lost his job within two weeks of taking the jump, dollarization in its early stages has turned out more successfully than almost anyone expected. However, the story is not yet over, and in the words of the IMF's unofficial motto, "complacency must be avoided."

I outline some of the key economic events and decisions leading up the dollarization decision, describe what has happened in the Ecuadorian economy since then, and note some of the challenges that the Ecuadorian government still faces.

Ecuador's economic history has not been a happy one. A lack

This is an edited version of a talk given at the Hoover Institution Conference on Currency Unions on May 19, 2000; the style reflects the informal nature of the original presentation. I am grateful to Tom Dawson, David Goldsbrough, John Thornton, and Robert Chote of the IMF for their advice and assistance. Views are those of the author and not necessarily of the IMF.

of national cohesion has dogged the country ever since it opted for independence from Simon Bolivar's Grancolombian Federation in 1830. From the start there was fierce rivalry between the residents of the highlands, centered on the capital Quito, and those on the coast, centered in Guayaquil. Fortunately, though, these rivalries did not lead to violent confrontation, and Ecuador's history, although turbulent, has been peaceful. However, the deep split between the interests of the coastal and highland regions has at times—and certainly during the last five years—made it almost impossible for the government to pursue a coherent economic policy.

In the mid-1990s, Ecuador's GDP was about $20 billion, with exports amounting to 20 percent of GDP. Half these exports were oil, which was discovered in the 1960s and came onstream in the 1970s. Bananas and shrimp were important too. By 1998 GDP had fallen to less than $18.5 billion, and by 2000 the massive overdepreciation of the currency had cut this to $13 billion—for a population of 12.5 million. In 2001 GDP will probably rise to more than $17 billion.

Ecuador's last good year economically was 1994, during the presidency of Sixto Duran Ballen. GDP grew by 4 percent and inflation was 27 percent. The Duran administration also decided to adjust gasoline prices monthly and automatically by indexing them to world prices. Up to that time, the adjustment of gasoline prices was always a potential political problem. However, in 1995, Ecuador fought a border war with Peru, increasing military spending and moving what had been an approximately balanced budget into significant deficit. The Duran administration lost credibility as the vice president, who had been a major force in economic policy, fled to Costa Rica to evade arrest on charges of corruption.

Popular discontent ushered in the colorful presidency of Abdala Bucaram—who was called El Loco—in the 1996 election. Bucaram came to office as a populist but almost immediately invited Domingo Cavallo to advise him. He seemed to be moving in the direction of

President Carlos Menem in Argentina—who came to office apparently a populist, only to institute a serious stabilization and reform program. After visiting Ecuador, Cavallo concluded that the country did not yet meet the preconditions necessary to institute a currency board successfully. President Bucaram lost credibility as a result of other actions, including alleged corruption and cronyism.

In February 1997 the situation deteriorated into a general strike, and in a last desperate bid for survival Mr. Bucaram undid some of the reforms he had implemented; he also stopped the indexation of energy prices. Eventually Mr. Bucaram found himself barricaded in his palace, and his Congress voted to remove him on grounds of "mental incapacity." For a brief confusing period three people claimed to be president: Mr. Bucaram, his vice president, and the leader of Congress. In the end it was the congressional leader Fabian Alarcón who was appointed interim president. Lacking authority and a clear mandate, he made no effort at reform and instead tried to bolster his popularity with concessions to unions and regional lobbies. More bad luck followed with, El Niño in 1997, which caused severe crop damage and destroyed infrastructure in the coastal region, at a total cost of about 13 percent of GDP.

The situation did not degenerate into a full-blown economic crisis during the Bucaram and Alarcón governments in part because private sector investors were still willing to finance emerging markets—particularly a country with oil—in the face of falling U.S. interest rates. Chase Manhattan gave Ecuador a $300 million bridging loan in December 1996, and—just three months after the ousting of President Bucaram—Ecuador managed to issue a $500 million eurobond. It is perhaps symbolic of the emerging market euphoria at the time that Moody's gave Ecuador the same credit rating as Brazil and Argentina—and this at a time when Ecuador was in arrears to its official creditors in the Paris Club.

When Jamil Mahuad was elected president in July 1998, it looked for a while as though things might change. Mr. Mahuad, a man of intelligence, charm and integrity, had established a reputation for reform during two terms as mayor of Quito. He took office in August 1998, and his authority in the country was enhanced when he signed a final peace agreement with Peru in October of that year. But it was during his presidency that the economy degenerated into crisis.

One problem was a rapidly deteriorating fiscal position. The public sector deficit ballooned from 2.6 percent of GDP in 1997 to 6.2 percent in 1998. Ecuador's external debt of more than $16 billion was also large relative to GDP. Three factors were crucial: revenue weakness from falling oil prices, the low nonoil tax base, and big public sector wage rises. The rapidly worsening condition of the banking system further complicated the situation. Action was needed urgently to reduce the deficit, allow lower interest rates, stop the accumulation of external arrears, and reduce debt service to sustainable levels. President Mahuad visited the IMF in September 1998 and explained that he preferred to manage without an IMF program.

By the time the IMF began the 1998 Article IV surveillance discussions in late September, the government had cut energy subsidies, raised gasoline prices, hiked interest rates, and devalued the exchange-rate band by 15 percent. But it was clear that much more had to be done. We argued that the fiscal deficit should be halved and expressed serious concern about the health of the banking system—noting a rise in nonperforming loans, the drying up of external credit lines, and too much lending in U.S. dollars to sucre-based borrowers. In response, the authorities explained the political barriers to fiscal tightening and said we were overstating the problems in the financial sector. Nonetheless, on October 2, the authorities said that they did want to negotiate an IMF-supported program.

We then entered an exceptionally long and difficult period of negotiation. IMF teams were in Quito at least half the time between November 1998 and March 2000; we had an agreement in September 1999 that did not work out; and we were ready to conclude another agreement in January 2000, just before dollarization.

There were two basic difficulties in the way of an agreement. First, recurrent banking sector problems were met through a series of ad hoc actions, including a deposit freeze in March 1999 and government bailouts typically carried out without consultation. Second, related fiscal problems made it difficult to get agreed programs implemented. Political and social problems prompted further counterproductive fiscal measures, for example, the replacement of the income tax with a financial transactions tax in November 1998.

By the time an IMF mission went to Ecuador in March 1999, the country's exchange-rate band had been abandoned after high interest rates and $250 million in intervention had failed to save it. The finance minister had also resigned after fiscal tightening measures were withdrawn from the budget before it was sent to Congress.

Nonetheless, this mission made some progress. The authorities sent a tax reform package to Congress that included the reinstatement of the income tax and a broadening of the VAT base. We also agreed on the principles of a bank resolution strategy. However, the resignation of the central bank president and three board members made it impossible to reach agreement on monetary policy. The authorities also continued to favor direct bailouts of favored banks with public money. When there was a run on the Banco Progreso, the second-largest bank in Ecuador (in terms of assets), the authorities declared a five-day bank holiday and froze all deposits and loans in the bank for a year.

Two months later, Congress had approved a weakened tax package and our team was back in Quito. Despite some progress, agreement on a full program again proved impossible. With the fiscal deficit still on course for 6 percent of GDP, the president refused to push for further tightening because of looming congressional elections. Energy price rises were rolled back and the authorities were not willing to submit legislation to protect the banking reform strategy from political interference.

By late June, we were embarked on our fourth mission visit in seven months. Agreement was reached on many elements of a program, including the main details of a banking strategy. But on this occasion the discussions were interrupted by social unrest, prompting the president to freeze energy prices for a year.

We finally reached agreement on a program in August, conditional on congressional approval for the tax strategy and progress in banking reform. We expected to finalize a program by October but knew that the Ecuadorians had significant interest payments to make on external debt in late September. The authorities asked us what they should do. We said that the decision was up to them: if they defaulted, then there was a risk of disruptive legal challenges; if they paid, it would be difficult to sustain a viable cash flow position.

In the end, the authorities delivered their Letter of Intent to the Fund on September 29, announcing on the same day that they were deferring interest payments due the following day on some of their Brady bonds. A little less than a month later, the Ecuadorians also announced they would not make a eurobond payment due on October 28 and unilaterally rescheduled part of their domestic dollar-denominated debt.

Throughout this period, public support for Mr. Mahuad was declining steadily from the peak of more than 60 percent he achieved in the wake of the peace agreement with Peru. With the sucre heading south rapidly—and Ecuador in the midst of a recession that would see output decline by more than 7 percent in 1999—frustration was mounting. The social impact of the country's problems was clear to see. The proportion of Ecuador's population in poverty reached almost 45 percent in 1999, up by a third since 1995. Meanwhile, unemployment had doubled to 17 percent since the beginning of 1998. In November and December the sense of crisis was heightened as inflation accelerated and the sucre's decline gathered pace.

Addressing the nation at the end of the year, the president promised a drastic change in course—only to see the sucre fall another 25 percent over the next few days. His approval rating plummeted with it, reaching just 7 percent. By the time Mr. Mahuad announced the decision to dollarize on January 9, the sucre had lost almost 80 percent of its dollar value in the sixteen months since he had taken office. The dollarization decision did produce some recovery in the president's poll rating, but it was one last blip. On January 21 he was ousted in a civilian-military coup.

The decision to dollarize was taken in desperation. The authorities did not consult with us, although they did take advice from some outside advisers including the Argentine consulting group, Mediterranea, and Guillermo Calvo. If they had asked us, we would have said that the preconditions for making a success of dollarization were not in place. In particular, the banking system was unhealthy and the fiscal position was weak.

However, once the decision to dollarize had been made, the best choice was to try to help it succeed: we spoke to the president and the finance minister on the day after the dollarization announcement and said that we would do what we could to help. Thereafter we have worked very closely with the Ecuadorian government, seeking to help them ensure that dollarization does succeed and that the stability it has brought so far (albeit not yet to prices) is maintained and strengthened.

President Mahuad's successor was the former vice president, Gustavo Noboa. He opted to stick with dollarization, reflecting the widespread conviction that all reasonable alternatives had now been exhausted. After demonstrations during which a group of indigenous peoples, with the support of some members of the army, occupied Congress (an event that drove home the need for national coherence), the administration also managed to muster support for a broad-based program of economic reform, symbolized by passage of the so-called trolleybus law through Congress. As a result our Executive Board was finally able to support Ecuador's program on April 19, approving a twelve-month standby credit of $304 million. With additional support from other multilateral lenders, this offered Ecuador around $900 million over the next twelve months, with up to $2 billion possibly available from official lenders over the next three years.

Given Ecuador's large external financing needs, it was clear that private sector creditors would have to play their part. The country needed both cash flow relief and debt reduction to secure a sustainable external and fiscal position for the medium term. In line with our existing policy, we were willing to lend to Ecuador while it was in arrears to its private creditors, on the basis of an agreed program and provided the country were engaged in good faith negotiations with the creditors. Ecuador managed to secure a successful debt exchange in August. Ecuador offered to exchange all of its Brady and eurobonds (with a combined face value of $6.5 billion) for a combination of new thirty-year and twelve-year bonds. Some 97 percent of all bondholders accepted the exchange offer, which gave Ecuador a substantial debt reduction (by about 40 percent of the face value of the bond debt) as well as significant cash flow relief in the initial years. In September, official Paris Club creditors agreed to grant Ecuador a rescheduling/deferral of about $800 million in arrears and maturities due in 2000.

Private sector players have criticized our approach to Ecuador's debt problems on a number of grounds. Some claim that the IMF bullied Ecuador into defaulting on its Brady debt last year. This is not true: we made it clear that private sector involvement would be necessary, but we did not advise them what to do about specific payments.

There is a grudging acceptance now among most market participants that some coordination—or coercion—of private sector creditors may be necessary on occasion to resolve financial crises. But there are still complaints that we are too vague about the approach we will take in particular cases. This is an unfortunate consequence of the fact that individual cases vary widely and that a flexible approach is essential. On most occasions, the combination of a robust policy program and short-term financial help from the fund should be enough to restore access to private capital markets. But more concerted action to coordinate creditors may be necessary if a country faces a large short-term financing requirement and has little hope of early access to capital markets—or if its medium-term debt profile looks unsustainable.

It is interesting to note that some market participants predicted that the sky would fall if this approach were followed. But debt reschedulings have taken place for both Ukraine and Pakistan without the disruptive litigation that many predicted.

The early (and largely unexpected) success of dollarization has helped restore confidence in the banking system, promoting a rise in bank deposits and an increase in bank reserves with the central bank. But indigenous groups remain wary of the policy, and it is not yet clear that the government has finally managed to assemble the durably stable legislative coalition that has so long eluded its predecessors. It is that stability that will rekindle confidence at home and abroad and lay the foundations for an enduring recovery from the country's torturous economic problems. These foundations should include a sensible tax reform so as to replace existing highly distortionary taxes (the financial transactions tax and an import tariff surcharge) and to avoid excessive reliance on oil revenues. They also include implementation of corporate debt restructuring in a manner that does not bail out large borrowers at taxpayers' expense and a comprehensive revamping of the financial sector. And both sustainable growth and a stable political situation will be more likely with policies that invest in critical social sectors.

There is much food for thought in the story of Ecuadorian dol-

larization—not least, that the early success of what was a desperation move, taken in haste, without most of what were thought of as
the necessary preconditions being in place, requires us to reconsider
the conditions under which such a switch in the monetary system
will succeed. But I should conclude with a final word of caution: it
is less than a year since the dollarization decision was taken, and
much work remains to be done to put in place a strong banking
system, the other monetary and fiscal institutions, and the political
consensus that will ensure the longer-term success of this remark-
able change in monetary regime.

Alberto Alesina
Robert J. Barro

2
One Country,
One Currency?

In 1947, there were 76 countries in the world; today there are 193. The largest country in the world (China) has 1.2 billion inhabitants; the smallest (Palau) has 16,600.[1] With few exceptions, a different currency circulates in every country, even the smallest ones.

Is each country an "optimal currency area" in the sense of Mundell (1961)? It is quite unlikely that the answer is yes for both China and Palau; it is also unlikely that the number of optimal currency areas happened to be around 70 in 1946 and about 180 today. In fact, the increasing amount of trade and financial integration suggests that the number of optimal currency areas may actually have fallen in the last few decades.

Partly as a result of the proliferation of many small countries,[2] the identification of one country, one currency has recently been called into question. An additional force pushing toward *dollari-*

---

1. Palau is the smallest country with a seat in the United Nations.
2. Currently the median country size is about 6 million.

zation (by which we mean the use by one country of another country's currency) has been a renewed emphasis on price stability. This emphasis was natural after an unfortunate decade (the 1980s) of exceptionally high inflation rates in many developing countries and double-digit inflation in many OECD countries.

Twelve countries in Europe have adopted a single currency, and a few others (the United Kingdom and Sweden) may enter soon (although Denmark recently declined). Ecuador is adopting the dollar. Argentina and Hong Kong employ a currency board with the U.S. dollar, and El Salvador decided to dollarize. In addition, a currency union for Central America is being considered. Estonia and Bulgaria had a currency board with the German deutsche mark and now with the euro, and several other eastern European countries are considering doing the same. Currency unions that were formed much earlier include the French franc zone in Africa, the Eastern Caribbean Currency Union, Panama with the United States, and a few others.

In our formal analysis (Alesina and Barro 2000), we discuss the pros and cons of adopting a foreign currency as the domestic currency. On the basis of this cost-benefit analysis, we try to characterize how many currency unions should exist in the world.

What are the benefits to a country from adopting the currency of a foreign anchor? First, a country pretty much secures the inflation rate of the anchor. Therefore, if the country lacks the discipline and credibility to keep inflation low and stable, dollarization buys a credible policy of price stability.

There are several reasons why most countries would have difficulty on their own in attaining price stability. One is a policymaker's temptation to use monetary expansion to counter recessions. If the policymaker can raise inflation above its expected level, there is some evidence that economic activity would be temporarily stimulated. However, since the public realizes the policymaker's intentions, this temptation tends to generate high and volatile inflation with no benefits in terms of expanded economic activity.[3] The reason is that inflation cannot systematically be above expected inflation, or, to paraphrase Abraham Lincoln, you cannot fool all of the people all of the time.

A second source of inflation is the fiscal pressure to monetize deficits. An unexpected burst of inflation reduces the real value of government debt denominated in domestic currency and, thereby, looks fiscally attractive to the government. However, knowing about this potential in advance, people bid up interest rates.

As a consequence, many countries in the 1970s and 1980s found themselves in suboptimal situations with high inflation and no benefits in terms of unemployment or fiscal revenues. In several cases, such as Argentina and Brazil, these situations degenerated into hyperinflation.

Fixed exchange rates were sometimes suggested as a cure for this problem. The idea is that the pegged nominal exchange rate would be an anchor that would limit the government's ability to inflate—because domestic inflation creates pressure for devaluation of the currency. The problem, however, is that the apparent commitment to fixed exchange rates can readily be broken, and this possibility generates speculative attacks and instability, as shown by recent experiences in Mexico, Brazil, and East Asia. In this respect, dollarization—or, in a less extreme version, a currency board—is far superior to a fixed exchange rate. A full dollarization is much harder to reverse and, therefore, ensures more credibility, lower risk premia, and greater financial stability.

The second benefit from dollarization involves the reduction in transaction costs for exchanges of goods and financial services across borders. By sharing the same currency, two countries economize on trading costs, and the larger the currency union, the larger the benefit. Money is like language—the more people speak the

3. See Barro and Gordon (1983) for a formal analysis of this problem.

same language, the easier it is to communicate; the larger the number of people sharing the same currency, the easier it is to trade.

Recent results by Rose (2000), summarized in this volume, suggest that the benefits of dollarization for trade may be quite large. Rose bases his empirical analysis on the performance of existing currency unions. His findings indicate that the sharing of a common currency may, holding other things equal, increase the volume of trade dramatically—by a factor of two to three. Although this effect is large, the magnitude accords with other empirical results that have identified a strong home bias in trade.[4] For instance, two Canadian provinces trade with each other much more than a Canadian province and a U.S. state, even after accounting for other empirical determinants of trade flows. To the extent that part of this home bias comes from sharing the same currency, one should expect large trade effects from currency unions. In addition, the home-bias phenomenon applies not only to trade but also to financial transactions.[5] Thus, adopting a currency union would also be likely to generate a large increase in cross-border financial transactions.

One frequently mentioned cost of adopting a foreign currency is the loss of an independent monetary policy for stabilization purposes. A country that dollarizes loses its ability to target its monetary policy to its own disturbances—instead, the country has to accept the policy chosen by the anchor. In principle, the cost from the lost independence is greater the less correlated a country's disturbances are with the anchor country. However, this cost may have been overstated in past discussions because it is unclear that many small, open, and developing countries actually have the ability to use independent monetary policies effectively for stabilization purposes. Many observers have raised serious doubts that developing

4. See McCallum (1995) and Helliwell (1998).
5. See Obstfeld and Rogoff (2000) for a theoretical discussion of the pervasive effects of home biases in international markets.

countries with floating exchange rates have been able to use the apparent flexibility in an efficient manner.[6]

A second cost emerges from movements in relative prices. Even if a country dollarizes, relative prices will still fluctuate. Therefore, the country's inflation rate would equal that of the foreign anchor plus the rate of change of the price of a basket of the country's goods expressed relative to that of the foreign country. Thus, price stability for the anchor does not translate exactly into price stability for its clients.

A third cost involves the loss of the seignorage revenue from a government printing its own paper money. However, this loss amounts to a redistribution from clients to anchor, rather than an overall cost. The seignorage could be returned, in full or in part, to the client.[7] In fact, the allocation of seignorage can be part of a larger compensation agreement between clients and anchor.

To understand the role of compensations, one should begin with the benchmark case in which the anchor country returns all the seignorage revenue to the dollarizing country. In this case, the anchor has no incentive to tailor its monetary policy to the interests of its clients. However, by allowing payments from the clients to the anchor, mutually beneficial transactions may occur. That is, a client may compensate the anchor for modifications of the anchor's monetary policy that reflect the client's interests. In this environment, the anchor would maximize an objective that assigns weights to the objectives of all members of the union.[8] The determination of the weights depends on country sizes and on the compensation

---

6. See Calvo and Reinhart (2000), which is discussed in this volume. However, Broda (2000), also summarized here, reaches different conclusions.

7. Note that a fully credible currency board can be viewed as a currency union in which the client retains the seignorage. However, moving from a currency board to a currency union may increase credibility because it is more costly to abandon the latter system than the former.

8. We can think of the European Central Bank as acting in this way.

schemes that are in place. In equilibrium, the allocation of transfers and the monetary policy of the anchor will depend on the composition of the group of clients and the correlation of their disturbances.

If compensations are feasible, then a small anchor is relatively cheap to buy. That is, a large client in search of a monetary anchor may find it advantageous to compensate a small but committed anchor. This consideration suggests that Switzerland would be a preferable anchor to the United States. Thus, it would be particularly profitable for a small country to specialize in providing the services of an anchor.

However, two other considerations may weigh in favor of large anchors. First, the reduction in trading costs is more significant the larger is the anchor. Second, the ability to commit may be dependent on size. Consider a large country, say Russia, attempting to link its currency to a small, disciplined country, such as Estonia. Ex post, the large country may pressure the small anchor to abandon its apparently committed policy. This possibility makes the arrangement less credible ex ante, so that the small country may not actually serve as a satisfactory anchor.

The argument about ex-post pressures to accommodate economic disturbances of the clients also highlights why potential anchors (such as the U.S. Federal Reserve and the European Central Bank) have been cautious in supporting unilateral adoptions of their currencies. They fear that economic crises in foreign countries will create pressures to accommodate foreign shocks, even if there are no formal obligations for these accommodations.

Finally, dollarization depends on good practice being maintained by the anchor country, for example, by the U.S. Federal Reserve or the European Central Bank. Policies in the United States and Europe have, in fact, been committed to low and stable inflation for some time—since the mid-1980s. There is some reason to believe that this state of affairs reflects permanent changes in knowledge about which monetary policies are effective and about how to achieve near price stability. However, dollarizing clients do take the risk of deteriorations in future policies.

In summary, the countries that are most likely to benefit from adopting a foreign currency are

1. Countries with an inability to achieve monetary and price stability on their own

2. Countries with economic disturbances that are highly correlated with those of the potential anchor

3. Small countries that are highly dependent on foreign trade

4. Countries that are close in distance to potential anchors and, therefore, could potentially trade a lot with the anchor

Given these considerations, we would expect the most likely currency unions to look as follows: one anchor country credibly committed to price stability provides the currency and the monetary policy for the union; clients are countries that are close to the anchor, small, and trade a lot with the anchor.

The size of the currency union is determined by a trade-off between scale and heterogeneity. As the size of the union increases with new entrants, more and more transaction costs of trade are saved. However, as the size of the union increases, the less the monetary policy of the anchor can be tailored to each member. The marginal entrant is the client that is so far from the anchor that its benefits from commitment and trade just compensate for a monetary policy that is little correlated with the entrant's disturbances. It should be noted that we use the term *distance* in the same way as the often used *gravity model* of international trade. This empirical model shows that countries trade more if they are close not only in miles but also if they share a common language, a border, a former colonizer, and so on.

Although the model sketched above is the most natural form of currency union, other types are also possible. For instance, a group of countries that lack a strong commitment to low inflation may choose to share a common currency to economize on trading costs. This situation is most likely to arise if a group of small countries trade heavily with one another, are close together, and are far from any potential anchor. The argument for a currency union in Central America seems to be based on this idea, although adoption of the U.S. dollar actually seems more promising.

The previous discussion suggests that, as the number of countries increases and their average size diminishes, the optimal number of currencies should increase less than proportionally to the number of countries. In fact, one can imagine cases in which, as the number of countries increases, the optimal number of currencies decreases. Consider the following example: three countries next to each other, with three currencies. Suppose that the middle country, which is the only one unable to commit to stable prices on its own, splits into two equally sized countries. The two new countries are smaller and, hence, more dependent on foreign trade. In addition, each of the two new countries is now closer geographically to one of the other two preexisting countries. It is, therefore, possible that the two new smaller countries would decide to adopt the currencies of the two larger and committed countries. The world has, therefore, moved from a situation of three countries and three currencies to a setting of four countries and two currencies.

This example highlights the point from which we started: the tendency to form a currency union is likely to increase as the number of independent countries increases, especially if these new countries are small and heavily dependent on international trade and financial integration. Probably the main factor that has retarded this tendency up to now is that, with few exceptions, countries seem politically highly attached to their individual currencies, perhaps as a symbol of national sovereignty. This behavior is somewhat puzzling, because many countries willingly share a common language, often the one of a former colonizer.

Currency unions are also politically charged because they affect regional integration and disintegration. If a country has joined a currency union, then the cost of separation to a region within the country will have diminished because the separated region can still benefit from the common currency of the union.[9] This point has been made with reference to regions of European countries in the euro area. Several commentators have noted that regional tensions within countries have been fueled by the monetary unification in Europe.

In summary, we suggest that it is unlikely that the optimal number of currency areas equals the actual number of circulating currencies, which currently is about 180. We have emphasized the trade-offs that should identify and determine the optimal number of currencies. Further empirical analysis, currently under way, can identify which groups of countries are attractive candidates for currency unions.

References

Alesina, A., and R. Barro (2000). "Currency Unions." Harvard University, unpublished. Presented at the Hoover Institution Conference on Currency Unions, May 2000, forthcoming in the *Quarterly Journal of Economics*.

Alesina A., E. Spolaore, and R. Wacziarg (2000). "Economic Integration and Political Disintegration." *American Economic Review*, forthcoming.

Barro, R., and D. Gordon (1983). "Rules, Discretion, and Reputation in a Model of Monetary Policy." *Journal of Monetary Economics*, July, 101–21.

Broda, C. (2000). "Terms of Trade and Exchange Rate Regimes in Developing Countries." Unpublished. Presented at the Hoover Institution Conference on Currency Unions, May 2000.

---

9. For a theortical and empirical discussion of the relationship between political and economic integration, see Alesina, Spolaore, and Wacziarg (2000).

Calvo, G., and C. Reinhart (2000). "Fear of Floating." University of Maryland, unpublished. Presented at the Hoover Institution Conference on Currency Unions, May 2000.

Helliwell, J. (1998). *How Much Do National Borders Matter?* Washington D.C.: Brookings Institution Press.

McCallum, J. (1995). "National Borders Matter: Canadian-U.S. Regional Trade Patterns." *American Economic Review*, June, 615–23.

Mundell, R. (1961). "A Theory of Optimum Currency Areas." *American Economic Review*, September, 651–65.

Obstfeld, M., and K. S. Rogoff (1996). *Foundations of International Macroeconomics.* Cambridge: MIT Press.

Rose, A. (2000). "One Money, One Market: Estimating the Effect of Common Currency on Trade." *Economic Policy*, forthcoming.

Charles Engel
Andrew K. Rose

3
Dollarization and Integration

Recently economists have developed considerable evidence that regions that are politically integrated also tend to be highly economically integrated. There is much more economic intercourse within political unions than between political unions. The volume of trade, the degree of business-cycle correlation, the linkage of prices of goods and services, the opportunities to insure economic risks—all are greatly enhanced within the member states of a political union compared to groups of independent political entities.

Although the facts about economic integration have been firmly established, the underlying causes for this "home bias" in integration are in dispute. Many hypotheses have been advanced. Formal and informal barriers to international trade, for example, might help explain why there is more economic interaction within countries than between countries. However, available evidence suggests that visible barriers to trade—such as tariffs or quotas—are inadequate to explain the greater level of linkages intranationally. Proposed explanations include the common laws and political environment;

the shared culture and language; and the shared history and so forth of units within political borders.

Here we investigate one possible explanation for the "border effect": households and firms within a country usually make transactions with a common currency. The British all use pounds, and the Japanese all use yen. But international transactions involve a swap of currencies. So the greater convenience from using the same currency might explain the high levels of integration of economies within a political union.

Currencies owe their existence to their ability to solve a problem of coordination among economic agents. The butcher might wish to buy a loaf of bread; the baker might want a candle; and, the candlestick maker would like a nice steak. How can the sellers and buyers be organized so that each can purchase the goods she wants? If there were no currencies, the three would need to meet and discuss how to arrange trade among them. Economists use the term *transactions costs* to label those costs associated with buying and selling products. But currencies coordinate demands and supplies without any need for formal organization. Each can sell her product and purchase her desired goods using money. The transactions costs are much lower.

So transactions that occur between economic agents within a country benefit from the use of a common currency. But international economic interaction does not usually take place with a common currency. An exchange of one currency for another is required; thus transactions costs are higher for international transactions. We observe, however, that in several instances international transactions do not require currency exchange. That is because there are several currency unions in existence around the world. A *currency union* is a group of countries that use the same currency. Examples are the CFA Franc zone and the East Carribean Currency Area. To the extent that economic transactions are facilitated by the use of a common currency, we expect to find greater economic linkages among countries of a currency union than among countries that do not share a common currency.

So our objective is to examine the economic linkages among currency union countries. Are they greater than the linkages for non–currency union members? Are the linkages as great as economists have found within political unions? The answers, in short, are yes and no, respectively.

We use several data sets for our study. The first data set consists of annual observations from 1960 to 1996 for 210 countries, territories, colonies, and other entities for many macroeconomic variables. The data are taken from the 1998 World Bank *World Development Indicators* and are extremely comprehensive. There are, however, many missing observations for variables of interest. The second data set consists of bilateral trade volumes for 166 countries, measured annually from 1970 through 1995. The data are extracted from the "World Trade Data Base," a recompilation of United Nations trade data. It contains observations for goods measured at the four-digit Standard International Trade Classification (SITC) level.

First, some descriptive statistics help to characterize currency union countries relative to the whole sample of countries. Member countries of currency unions are smaller (in population) than most countries, and are poorer. Their average gross domestic product (GDP) per person is about one-third below the world average. They have on average had much lower inflation than non–currency unions. This is primarily because no currency union country in our sample ever experienced very high inflation (for example, over 50 percent per year), while such inflation rates are quite common in our overall sample. Real growth rates in currency union countries have not been appreciably higher than in non–currency union countries. Countries that are members of currency unions appear to be more open to international trade and capital flows. Their exports and imports (as a percentage of GDP) are about one-third greater than for our entire sample of countries; gross foreign direct investment (as a percentage of GDP) is about one-third greater; and private capital flows (again as a percentage of GDP) are about 80 percent greater. Although the growth rate of currency union countries has been no greater than for other countries, Frankel and Rose find that the openness of the currency union members is a significant channel for growth.[1]

Another characteristic of currency unions is that the members are more specialized in production and exports. By *specialization*, we mean the degree to which exports are concentrated in a narrow range of products. We use a standard measure of specialization, the Herfindahl index. Indeed, the members of currency unions are significantly more specialized than countries that have their own currencies. It might be objected that currency union members are smaller and poorer than other countries, so that more specialization is to be expected. But we control for factors such as GDP per capita and country size, and currency union members consistently have a higher degree of specialization. Succinctly, members of currency unions are more open than countries with their own currencies, and they are also more specialized.

We then turn to the question of whether currency unions really trade more than other countries, taking into account the size, income, and geographic remoteness of the currency union members. The gravity model of international trade has been a very successful predictor of the volume of trade between two countries. It points to distance between the two countries, income levels, and country size as being the most critical determinants of bilateral trade flows. Our data confirm that result. Using data for 1995 trade volumes for 150 countries and other political units, we estimate the gravity model of international trade. Greater distance between two countries lowers

---

1. Jeffrey Frankel and Andrew K. Rose, 2000, "An Estimate of the Effect of Currency Unions on Trade and Growth," paper delivered at Hoover Institution conference on Currency Unions, May.

trade, while greater economic *mass* (proxied by real GDP and real GDP per capita) increases trade.

But even after taking out the effects of output, size, and distance, there is a large effect of a common currency on trade. According to our estimates, two countries that share a common currency trade together by a factor of 6.5 more than two countries with separate currencies! This strong result is surprising, but it stands up to a number of tests for specification. We take into account the effects of being partners in a regional trade agreement, sharing a common language, having the same (post-1945) colonizer, being part of the same nation (as, for example, France and an overseas department like French Guiana), and having had a colonizer-colony relationship. All these factors increase trade by economically and statistically significant amounts. Also, landlocked and large countries tend to trade less, and islands trade more. But, even controlling for all of these other explanations for the volume of trade between nations, we find that sharing a common currency has a large and statistically significant effect on the volume of bilateral trade. Our lowest estimate indicates that trade is 285 percent higher for members of a currency union than for countries with sovereign currencies. This result is only strengthened when we pool the 1995 data together with data from 1970, 1975, 1980, 1985, and 1990.

Although our estimate of the intensity of trade within currency unions is provocatively high, it is actually quite low compared with the well-documented size of home bias in international trade. For example McCallum[2] and Helliwell[3] find the volume of trade between two regions within a country (controlling for distance, size, income, etc.) to be twelve to twenty times larger than the volume of trade between two regions that are located in different countries.

2. John McCallum, 1995, "National Borders Matter: Canada-U.S. Regional Trade Patterns," *American Economic Review* 85, no. 3: 615–23.

3. John Helliwell, 1998, *How Much Do National Borders Matter?* (Washington, D.C.: Brookings).

Although membership in a common currency area does intensify trade, it does not intensify it nearly enough for common currency areas to resemble countries.

Areal exchange rate is a measure of relative price levels between two countries. The price of a basket of goods in one country is divided by the price in another country, after first converting the prices into a common currency using the exchange value of one country's currency in terms of the other's. The latter is referred to as the *nominal exchange rate*. When nominal exchange rates are volatile, as they are for many countries with no controls on foreign exchange markets, the real exchange rate consequently tends to be volatile. Since currency union members use the same currency, their nominal exchange rate is fixed at one for one. With no nominal exchange-rate volatility, we might expect to find greater real exchange-rate stability within currency unions.

Obstfeld and Rogoff[4] discuss two of the benefits from currency unions, relating to real exchange-rate stability. First, accounting costs are reduced and the greater predictability of relative prices reduces uncertainty for firms doing business in the countries of a currency union. Second, the currency union countries are not subject to the fluctuations in nominal exchange rates caused by monetary disturbances and speculative bubbles that lead to temporary unnecessary fluctuations in real exchange rates.

We measure real exchange-rate stability in two ways. The first is a measure of how quickly real exchange rates adjust to sudden disturbances. The second is simply a measure of the overall volatility—the standard deviation of annual percentage changes in the real exchange rate. We use annual data on real exchange rates from 1960 to 1996.

As to the first measure, we simply find no evidence of faster

---

4. Maurice Obstfeld and Kenneth Rogoff, 1996, *Foundations of International Macroeconomics* (Cambridge, Mass.: MIT Press).

adjustment within currency unions compared to countries with their own currencies. But perhaps this is not too surprising if the disturbances to currency union real exchange rates are much smaller than those that hit countries with sovereign currencies. Perhaps there is a great deal of transitory real exchange-rate volatility associated with volatile nominal exchange rates. When disturbances to nominal exchange rates are large and lead to large misalignments of real exchange rates, there may be rapid adjustment.

Indeed, we do find using our second measure that the standard deviation of real exchange rates is lower for currency union members. Every 10 percentage-point drop in the standard deviation of nominal exchange rates leads to approximately a 4 percentage-point drop in the standard deviation of real exchange rates. So the elimination of nominal exchange rate volatility can contribute significantly to the reduction in instability in real exchange rates. Moreover, even controlling for nominal exchange-rate volatility, real exchange rates appear to be more stable within currency unions. Being a member of a currency union reduces the standard deviation of annual real exchange rates by 6 percentage points relative to countries with sovereign currencies.

It appears that much of the success in reducing real exchange-rate volatility in currency unions is attributable to the elimination of high inflation. When inflation is high, it also tends to induce a lot of relative price-level fluctuations between countries. Low-inflation countries with sovereign currencies have real exchange-rate volatility that is only modestly higher than that of currency union members. Moreover, relative price volatility between countries within currency unions appears to be significantly greater than relative price volatility between cities within political unions. We can again conclude that common currency areas are not as integrated as political unions.

Another dimension of integration of economies is the comovement of GDP. Do countries with a common currency have more highly synchronized business cycles? We compute the correlation of output movements in countries, both for currency union countries and for countries with their own currencies, using annual data on GDP for 1960–1996. We find that the correlation coefficients tend to be perhaps .1 higher on average for currency union members than for nonmembers. This finding is robust when we include controls for country size, regional trade agreements, common language, sharing a common border, and so on. Although economically and statistically significant, the size of this effect is small in an absolute sense.

Most recently, Clark and van Wincoop[5] have compared the coherence of business cycles within countries and across countries, using annual data for both employment and real GDP. They show that intranational business-cycle correlations are apporximately .7 for regions within countries but in the range of .2 to .4 for comparable regions across countries. That is, the effect of international borders on business-cycle synchronization ranges between .3 and .5. Thus, only a small part of the border effect is explained by membership in a common currency area.

We have seen that international capital flows tend to be greater among currency union members than among nonmembers (as a percentage of GDP). One of the benefits of international trade in assets is that it allows for diversification to protect against risks to income. The most comprehensive measure of how well individuals can diversify risk is to measure how protected consumption levels in a country are from income shocks. When households can fully diversify risk internationally, consumption should be independent of idiosyncratic income shocks within a country.

However, we find that there is no increase in consumption "insurance" among currency union members relative to countries with

5. Todd E. Clark and Eric van Wincoop, 2000, "Borders and Business Cycles," Federal Reserve Bank of New York working paper.

their own currencies. We use annual data on consumption and GDP from 1960 to 1992. We find that consumption in currency union countries is no more insulated from domestic income shocks than in other countries. This stands in contrast to evidence that there is a great deal of risk sharing among regions within countries. But much of the risk sharing that occurs within political unions occurs through fiscal transfers (taxes and redistribution), rather than through diversification by private agents. Moreover, financial markets remain underdeveloped in most currency union countries, so the opportunities for risk sharing are limited.

Although members of international currency unions are more integrated than countries with their own monies, they remain far from integrated compared with the intranational benchmark of regions within a country. Home bias is pervasive. Goods, labor, and capital markets are all much more integrated within national borders than across national borders. Some economists believe that this border effect is largely the result of national monies. In this paper we have found that a national money is a significant but small part of the national economic institutions that create this home bias.

Jeffrey A. Frankel
Andrew K. Rose

4

An Estimate of the Effect of Currency Unions on Trade and Growth

Many countries are, for the first time, considering the possibility of abandoning independent currencies and adopting rigid institutional commitments, including currency boards (Argentina and Estonia), dollarization (El Salvador and Ecuador), or full currency union (the members of the European Monetary Union). Proponents tout such currency arrangements as the ultimate credible commitment to nonexpansionary monetary policy. The idea is that when the central bank ties its hands so it could not in the future expand the money supply even if it wanted to, workers expect lower inflation. As a result, the country achieves lower inflation for any given level of output. Indeed, in the long run, the enhanced monetary stability promotes higher real economic growth. One study, for example, finds that currency boards raise long-term growth by as much as 1.8 percent per year.

We find that currency unions are indeed good for the performance of the economy in the long run, as indicated by a statistical association with economic growth. The channel, however, runs via a substantial stimulus to trade among the members, rather than via macroeconomic influences. In theory, as well as according to statistical evidence, trade is good for growth, and this is as true of trade that is stimulated by currency unions as of other sources of trade. This paper investigates both stages: the influence of currency unions on trade and the influence of trade on growth.

Currency unions go beyond reducing the variability of bilateral exchange rates. They eliminate altogether the risk of future changes in the exchange rate, as well as the transactions costs incurred from converting one currency into another. Thus they facilitate imports and exports. Past studies have not been able to find major effects over time of exchange-rate variability on trade. But by focusing on a cross-section of country pairs, we are able to find a large effect of currency unions. We estimate that when one country adopts the currency of another, trade between them eventually triples in magnitude.

We arrive at this estimate by studying trade between pairs of countries. We use the gravity model, so-called because it says that trade between two countries is inversely related to the distance between them and proportionate to the product of their sizes, much as the gravitational attraction between two heavenly bodies is inversely related to the distance between them and proportionate to the product of their masses. The model has been successful at predicting trade patterns. Measures of distance that are relevant for trade between a pair of countries include physical distance, measures related to adjacency and whether they are landlocked, and linguistic differences. Each has strong negative effects on trade. Measures of country size that are relevant are GDP, population, and land area.

After holding constant for all these important determinates, we can discern the independent effect on bilateral trade that comes when the two partners share a common currency. We also hold constant for past colonial history and ongoing political unions. Like the other gravity variables, these influences are significant statistically, but the independent effect of the currency union remains as well.

Our data to study bilateral trade include 41,678 bilateral trade observations—drawn from pairs among 186 countries, including in this definition of *country* dependencies, territories, overseas departments, and colonies. The data set spans six different years between 1970 and 1995. (Our growth equation uses a data set of annual observations for 210 countries.)

The threefold effect of currency unions on trade that we find sounds very large, and indeed it is. But it becomes plausible when one recalls findings that Canadian provinces are twelve to twenty times more inclined to trade with each other than with U.S. states, after holding constant for distance and size. Something has to explain such findings of "home country bias." The currency difference is as good a candidate as any other explanation. Our results show that among components of home bias, the currency union variable ranks in explanatory power roughly equal with the role of free trade areas, behind the colonial relationship, and ahead of linguistic links and the residual political boundary variable.

We checked whether the stimulus to trade between members of a currency union might come at the expense of trade with nonmembers. Such a diversion of trade away from nonmembers would imply less overall stimulus to total trade and less likelihood of positive effects on real income. We found no evidence whatsoever of trade diversion from currency unions. Indeed, we found that countries that belong to currency unions have higher overall openness, as measured by the ratio of trade to GDP, by 14 percent, as compared to countries that do not. (This estimate again holds constant for domestic size and income, along with overall remoteness from trading partners, and dummy variables such as landlockedness.) The foregoing estimate, however, does not take into account whether the country in question shares the currency of a large trading partner or a small one.

The next stage in our analysis is to investigate the effect of trade on growth. The proposition that trade has a positive effect on real income is almost as old as economic theory itself. It derives from the principle of comparative advantage. More recently, trade theorists have studied how an increase in trade might potentially have more than a onetime effect on the level of real income; it might raise the rate of economic growth on a long-term basis. Intensive economic interaction with the rest of the world speeds innovation and the adoption of new ideas, adding to growth in technological and managerial know-how and productivity.

Many empirical studies have confirmed a statistical relationship across countries between openness and the level or growth rate of real income. This is true even after holding constant for such other important determinants of growth as investment in physical capital (plant and equipment), investment in human capital (schooling), and initial income (the convergence phenomenon, whereby countries that start further behind have the potential to catch up).

Correlation does not necessarily imply causality, however. Trade may be correlated with growth because richer countries trade more, rather than the other way around. This is the problem of simultaneity: growth causes trade, while simultaneously trade causes growth. For example, countries tend to reduce tariffs as they become more developed. If a country engages in a lot of trade because it has low tariffs, the observed correlation with growth could be attributable to an effect of growth on tariffs and thereby on trade. Our statistical method for getting around this problem isolates that variation in trade that is specifically attributable to the exogenous influences captured by the gravity model. The influence of trade on growth turns out to be as strong or stronger when this technique is used, which we believe is free from the simultaneity problem. If a country engages in a lot of trade because it is located close to other large countries, the observed correlation with growth cannot be attributed to an effect of growth on location and trade. It must be because higher trade leads to growth.

We seek to explain 1990 income per capita across countries. We begin by holding constant only for country size (as measured by population). We estimate an apparent correlation whereby each increase in the trade/GDP ratio (which we are calling openness) of 1 percentage point is associated with an increase in per capita income of 0.7 percent. But the openness variable may in part be standing in for a host of other variables. So we hold constant for 1970 income per capita, investment, two measures of schooling, and population growth. Controlling for these influences brings the coefficient on trade down to 0.25, which says that, holding constant for 1970 income, income in 1990 was 0.25 percent higher for every 1.0 percentage point increase in the trade/GDP ratio.

The equation also implies a process of partial convergence of income levels over twenty years, estimated at a speed equal to one-quarter of the total distance from the 1970 starting point to the long-run equilibrium. It follows that in the truly long run, the effect of a currency union on income is four times as large as the 1990 effect.

This estimate is still subject to the critique that it might reflect reverse causation, of income on trade. Our preferred way of addressing the simultaneity problem is to focus on a measure of trade that is built up from the bilateral predictions of the gravity model. When the trade coefficient is estimated with this technique, as already noted, it is at least as strong as when it is estimated without it. Every 1 percentage-point increase in openness is estimated to raise the level of income by an estimated 0.33 percent, over the twenty-year period. In the truly long run, the effect on income is again four times as large: 1.3 percent for every 1 percentage point of trade/GDP.

Finally, we combine our estimated effect of currency unions on trade with our estimated effect of trade on growth to derive a combined prediction of the effect of currency unions on growth. Our predictions are based on the estimate that currency unions triple trade among the members. But the question of the ultimate effect should depend on who is adopting what currency. For example, our statistics imply generally that dollarization should raise an average country's income by roughly 4 percent over twenty years. But the answer varies according to whether or not the country in question is a natural trading partner of the United States.

El Salvador and Ecuador trade a lot with the United States, relative to their GDPs. The reasons are that they are small, the United States is large, and the distance is not great. As a consequence, our estimate is that dollarization should have a sufficiently large effect on the overall trade undertaken by El Salvador or Ecuador that it could raise their incomes by as much as 20 percent over the subsequent twenty-year period. But these countries trade much less with Europe, so that adopting the euro would have less effect on their overall trade and would thus be of less benefit to them. Conversely, Poland trades a lot with Western Europe, so that adopting the euro would subsequently raise income an estimated 20 percent, while dollarizing would have much less benefit. (In each of these three examples, trade with the regional hegemon is about half of the country's total trade. This implies that tripling the trade with the hegemon doubles the country's total trade.)

It is possible that our results, which we attribute to the bilateral trade channel, are in part due to other economic interactions that run along geographic lines that are similar to trade—investment, communication, migration. But we do offer evidence against the conventional belief that the long-term growth effects of currency unions come through macroeconomic influences. This follows from a demonstration of support for the hypothesis that the effects depend on the members being natural trading partners. We find no sign that simply belonging to a currency union in itself has any effect on a country's growth, beyond the effect achieved when the link is to major trading partners. Thus, it seems that the growth benefits do not come through the central bank credibility route but rather through the trade route.

An implication for policy of the usual hypothesis—that the benefits come via monetary stability—would be that it does not much matter to what country one pegs one's currency, as long as it is to a country with a currency that is strong and stable in value. A conclusion from our analysis, however, is that geography belongs in the decision to whom one should link. Countries tend naturally to trade more with large neighbors; thus, the benefits to adopting the currency of a large neighbor, other things equal, will exceed the benefits to adopting the currency of a country that is smaller or more distant.

The analysis is subject to many qualifications. For one thing, our sample of currency union members tends to consist of small dependencies. We cannot be confident that the results generalize to large countries like the members of the European Monetary Union. (Indeed, the spirit of the paper is that countries that are too small to achieve economies of scale domestically are particularly dependent on the benefits of economic interaction through currency unions and trade.) For another thing, although we have held constant for many influences, there may be others that we have not yet captured. Finally, we do not know if the beneficial effects of currency unions on trade come quickly or might appear only with very long lags.

Guillermo A. Calvo
Carmen M. Reinhart

5
Reflections on Dollarization

During the past few years, many emerging-market countries have suffered severe currency and banking crises. A popular view blames fixed exchange rates—specifically, soft pegs—for these financial meltdowns. Indeed, fixed exchange rates have been so demonized by some adherents to that view that the only alternative for emerging markets seems to be to allow their currencies to float.

Other analysts draw a very different lesson from these events. After all, a country cannot have a currency crisis if it does not have a domestic currency in the first place; firms, banks, and households are immune to currency mismatches if all assets and liabilities are denominated in the same currency. The obvious policy recommendation that follows is that full dollarization may, in some cases, be desirable. Some observers forecast that intermediate exchange-rate regimes will vanish, as countries move toward corner solutions—with freely floating exchange-rate regimes at one end and hard pegs, such as currency boards or dollarization, at the other. Thus, the current circumstances provide the ingredients for a rich policy debate.

Fear of Floating

On the surface, at least, a polarization in exchange-rate arrangements appears to be taking place. Eleven countries in Europe chose to give up their national currencies, whereas Ecuador was the first of what may be several countries in Latin America to adopt the United States dollar as its official national tender. At the other end of the spectrum, Korea, Thailand, Brazil, Russia, Chile, Colombia, and, more recently, Poland have announced their intentions to allow their currencies to float. On the basis of labels, at least, it appears that the new millennium will be very different as far as currency arrangements are concerned.

Yet a careful reading of the evidence on exchange-rate policy presents a strikingly different picture. Announcements of intentions to float are not new. The Philippines announced it would float in 1988—less than ten years later, its exchange-rate policy would be classified, together with the rest of the Asian crisis countries, under the commonly used (but ill-defined) label of a soft peg. Bolivia announced it would float on September 1985 owing to its hyperinflation—yet its exchange rate so closely tracked the United States dollar that the regime was reclassified as a *managed* float in January 1998. Korea and Thailand, despite their floating status, are amassing foreign exchange reserves at the time of this writing. If they are floating, they are doing so with a life jacket. After all, a floating exchange-rate arrangement should obviate the need for countries to maintain a war chest of reserves.

Is the middle disappearing? We don't think so. Empirical evidence suggests that *fear of floating* is pervasive, particularly among emerging markets. In a recent study,[1] we found that the currencies of emerging-market economies are less likely to fluctuate than those of the major industrial countries. The supposedly disappearing middle accounts for the lion's share of country practices. Indeed, one of the hardest challenges for policymakers trying to draw lessons from the experiences of countries that are at the corners is that hardly any countries are there to study. The experiences of some of the floaters, such as the United States and Japan, are not relevant for emerging markets. Similarly, the countries that have eschewed having their own currency are so few in number that it is difficult to draw generalized conclusions.

The reality is that any exchange rate that moves at all is now being labeled as a *floating exchange rate*. In truth, these floating exchange-rate regimes are far removed from what is classically defined as a floating exchange rate. One change that does appear to be taking place is that interest-rate policy is replacing foreign exchange intervention as the preferred means of smoothing exchange rates. This is evident in the high variability of interest rates in emerging markets and in the practices of countries such as Mexico and Peru. Does this change make countries less vulnerable to currency crises? It is possible but not probable. Interest-rate policy will have its limits (just as international reserves have their limit), as interest-rate hikes to defend the currency take their toll on the economy and the financial sector. All that we can say is that, when it comes to exchange-rate policy, discretion rules the day!

Where does this leave us? Because the experience with dollarization or floating is so limited that a definitive assessment at this stage is foolhardy, in what follows we will focus on how to think about these issues.

---

1. See Calvo and Reinhart (2000), "Fear of Floating," NBER Working Paper 7993, November.

Liability Dollarization

As noted, many analysts concluded that the soft pegs were responsible for the crises. At some level, the statement is right because, if the exchange rate were allowed to float freely, by definition some of the international reserve loss would have been prevented. However, such a characterization is incomplete. It misses a key point, namely, that, in these episodes, either the government or the private sector or both had large foreign exchange–denominated short-term debt obligations that exceeded the stock of international reserves. Therefore, it is probable that the currency crises would have taken place even under more flexible exchange-rate arrangements. This brings us to the issue of liability dollarization.

A common misconception in the ongoing debate about dollarization is that it is a drastic measure, requiring, among other things, the surrender of the central bank's ability to function as lender of last resort. But dollarization may not be the sharp departure from existing practices that its critics assume. Partial dollarization is well under way in emerging markets, particularly those that have a history of high inflation. Analysis of this issue typically focuses on deposit (asset) dollarization, but debt (liability) dollarization is equally important and far more widespread—even in countries with an admirable inflation track record. Individual borrowers with foreign exchange–denominated debts not matched by foreign exchange assets can be forced into bankruptcy by an unexpected depreciation of the exchange rate. The presence of such currency mismatches may argue for full dollarization.

It is possible that liability dollarization is partly a result of pegging, magnified by the overconfidence and moral hazard problems that pegging may bring about. As the argument usually goes, if the exchange rate were allowed to float, domestic investors would shy away from foreign exchange–denominated debts because they would face a larger currency risk than under a fixed exchange rate.

This argument sounds convincing, but it misses two important points: (1) most emerging markets start from a situation of partial dollarization (at the very least, liability dollarization), and (2) it is hard to find examples of an emerging market ignoring exchange-rate volatility. These points reinforce each other. Partial dollarization increases the cost of exchange-rate volatility, which, in turn, induces the central bank to intervene in the foreign exchange markets to prevent fluctuations in the nominal exchange rate. In fact, as the cases of Egypt, El Salvador, the Philippines, and Venezuela attest, this fear of floating may be so severe that the exchange rate spends long stretches of time at a fixed level, making it observationally equivalent to a soft peg. In turn, fear of floating induces more liability dollarization, creating a vicious circle from which it is difficult to exit. Fear of floating also arises from domestic firms' use of imported raw materials and may also drive authorities to adopt additional measures, such as controls on capital mobility. Even when fear of floating does not lead to capital controls, and countries adopt "market-friendly" ways of stabilizing the exchange rate through domestic open market operations, such policies have costs in terms of the interest-rate volatility associated with them as well as their procyclical nature. Thus, contrary to the view that floating provides authorities with an extra degree of freedom to guarantee a market-friendly environment, the opposite may happen.

Ineffective Lender of Last Resort

Another popular view is that the adoption of a currency board or dollarization significantly detracts from the central bank's ability to operate as lender of last resort. This view is based on the conjecture that, since the sums involved in bank bailouts are usually huge, an effective lender of last resort should be able to issue its own money.

True, a bank's liabilities are more liquid than its assets, which is why it is susceptible to runs. A possible way to prevent self-fulfilling bank runs is for the central bank to step in and bail out the banking system if a run takes place. If expected by the public, the bailout may never have to be activated, thus making lender of last resort capabilities costless to the central bank and beneficial to the private sector. However, this explanation of bank runs was formulated in terms of a nonmonetary economy. If the government's promise is to be credible, the government has to be able to finance the bailout. At its heart, this is a fiscal issue because, given the sums involved, this financing normally requires issuing government debt, which will eventually be serviced by higher taxes. Yet this may not be possible for an emerging market that has lost access to international capital markets.

Furthermore, this analysis does not address the issue of whether relinquishing the issuance of one's own money could impair the effectiveness of the lender of last resort. Suppose that deposits are denominated in domestic currency and that the central bank guarantees that depositors will be able to withdraw all their deposits, if they so wish. Would this insurance be effective in preventing self-fulfilling bank runs? Not at all—not if this policy does not ensure depositors that their deposits' purchasing power will remain intact. Consider the case in which bank deposit interest rates are subject to a statutory ceiling. If depositors expect the currency to weaken substantially, there will be a bank run that the government cannot stop by issuing money—indeed, issuing money will worsen the currency crisis. This example may not be relevant in economies where a large share of deposits earn interest. In this case, banks could stop the run by offering higher interest rates on their deposits or by indexing deposits to prices or the exchange rate. The latter (i.e., "dollarization" of deposits) is a popular practice in emerging markets. If higher interest rates are successful in stopping runs, a lender of last resort would not be needed because this operation could be undertaken by the banks without the help of the central bank. However, we cannot be hopeful about the high-interest strategy because rates may have to rise to the point that banks will go bankrupt (and we should not forget the adverse-selection problem). In a market economy where information is limited, depositors might interpret an individual bank's increase in its deposit rate as evidence of higher risk. Banks would fail either because interest rates on their liabilities rise substantially more than on their assets or because their loans become nonperforming.

Indexation provides a mechanism to raise deposit interest rates implicitly when expectations of a run arise. However, indexation increases the burden on the lender of last resort because deposits are now denominated in real terms. Indeed, if all deposits are indexed to the exchange rate, there would not be a major difference between this case and full dollarization.

Why do advanced countries manage to have an effective lender of last resort? The answer suggested above is simple: advanced countries never lose access to capital markets. Was it critical for those countries to be able to print their own currencies? We doubt it. Thus, contrary to popular belief, full dollarization may not entail a substantial loss of lender-of-last-resort capabilities in countries that are credit constrained.

The "Sudden Stop" Problem

Any discussion of exchange-rate options needs to give full weight to the environment in which that policy will be implemented. This analysis requires a discussion of the characteristics of international capital markets. As the debt crisis of the 1980s was resolved, official capital flows to emerging markets shrank and private capital flows assumed an increasingly important role. But, time and again, such flows have proved to be moody and fickle throughout the 1990s. Indeed, emerging markets routinely face what we call the "sudden stop" problem, that is, the immediate drying up of access to world financial markets. When a sudden stop occurs, the effects on the economy can be devastating.

Some analysts have suggested that the very increase in capital mobility in the past decade and the limited resources that central banks can muster, relative to the private sector, are a call for governments to allow their currencies to float. But this recommendation misses a key point: when capital leaves an emerging market abruptly, it entails a massive swing in a key relative price in a small open economy—the real exchange rate—with usually devastating consequences for the domestic economy and financial sector. Thus, few (if any) central banks in emerging markets would turn a blind eye to such sharp swings in the nominal (and real) exchange rate. The widespread incidence of fear of floating attests to this fact.

Yet it is certainly true that capital markets have become increasingly integrated and that central banks command limited resources. In our view, these observations suggest that central banks in most emerging markets are powerless to fend off a speculative attack, act as an effective lender of last resort, or *conduct independent monetary policy*, as the latter will be subjugated to accommodating the whims of the international capital markets. This, of course, implies that monetary policy will tighten when a sudden stop problem threatens (which is usually when the domestic economy is facing a slump or an adverse shock and would most benefit from low interest rates). In this environment, it is not clear what benefits an emerging market derives from having its own central bank and its own currency.

Capital in emerging markets has been moving with an intensity not seen since the late nineteenth and early twentieth centuries. This dynamism suggests that a system of fixed exchange rates (i.e., hard pegs)—like the gold standard system of that earlier era—may again be appropriate for emerging markets.

To Fix or Not to Fix

In summary, much of the glitter of flexible exchange rates disappears on closer examination. The extra degrees of freedom provided by exchange-rate flexibility are fallacious or can be substituted by fiscal policy. A point to remember in the debate over whether dollarization is appropriate for emerging markets is that these economies are still "emerging." They are setting policy in a world in which their own financial markets remain underdeveloped, their trade is invoiced predominantly in dollars, their corporate and financial institutions have a limited ability to hedge exchange-rate risk, and their governments, more often than not, lack credibility. Exchange-rate movements are costly in this environment. If policymakers take a hard look at the options for exchange-rate regimes in emerging economies, they may find that floating regimes may be more of an illusion and that fixed rates—particularly full dollarization—might emerge as a sensible choice for some countries, especially in Latin America or in the transition economies on the periphery of euroland.

Christian Broda

6
Coping with Terms of Trade Shocks: Pegs versus Floats

The choice of the exchange-rate regime has always been an area of great controversy and debate. The discussion has once again taken center stage in the developing world. The sequence of currency crises in the 1990s, the success of currency board arrangements, the dollarization plan of Ecuador, and the apparent swing toward flexible regimes in many emerging economies have revived interest in this debate.

Following the works of Robert Mundell and William Poole in the 1960s, many economists still believe that the relative merits of exchange-rate regimes depend on the nature of the shocks that buffet the economy. When shocks come from the domestic money market, fixed-rate regimes automatically prevent them from affecting the real economy. Money supply will increase as the monetary authority buys foreign reserves to prevent the appreciation of the local currency, and real output is left unchanged. In contrast, flexible-rate regimes require income to fall so that real money demand is reduced back to the unchanged level of real money supply. Therefore, if these shocks predominate in the economy, this is an argument in favor of fixed-rate regimes.

However, when shocks are mostly real, floats are in theory the more effective choice. Indeed, one of the most important benefits commonly attributed to fully floating exchange-rate regimes is that they allow smooth adjustment to real shocks. When domestic prices are sticky and thus change at best slowly in response to shocks, a negative real shock—say, a fall in export demand or in the terms of trade—leads to a depreciation of the nominal exchange rate.[1] This depreciation in the exchange rate, in turn, reduces the price of the tradable goods at precisely the moment that demand for them has fallen and therefore partially offsets the effect of the negative shock. That is, the exchange rate acts as an automatic stabilizer in flexible-rate regimes.

On the other hand, fixed-rate regimes have to rely on the slow changes of domestic prices to be pulled out from the recession. In other words, pegs simply have to live with the effects of the negative shocks. Moreover, the central bank must prevent the currency depreciation that would otherwise occur by buying domestic money with foreign currency. This response is inherently contractionary and induces an additional fall in employment. The long and agonizing deflationary periods necessary to realign relative prices in the United Kingdom and Argentina during, respectively, the 1920s and 1990s serve as reminders of the costs associated with a fixed nominal exchange rate.

Given the prominent role played by exchange-rate regimes in developing countries and the extent to which this choice of regimes is dictated by the issues elucidated above, it is perhaps surprising that there is scant empirical work addressing the relevance of these

---

1. As goods demand and output fall, the demand for money also falls. To maintain the money market in equilibrium, the nominal interest rate has to fall, which causes the domestic currency to depreciate in the foreign exchange market.

theories. Here I look at a post–Bretton Woods sample of seventy-four developing countries to test whether flexible regimes can buffer terms-of-trade shocks better that fixed regimes.

First, I classify countries by exchange-rate regime. The basic reference for classification of the exchange-rate regimes is provided by the International Monetary Fund. The IMF classification is de jure, based on the publicly stated commitment of the authorities in each country. This information captures the notion of a formal commitment to a regime but fails to consider whether the actual policies were consistent with this commitment. For example, take Central America in the mid-1980s: El Salvador (1983–84), Guatemala (1986–88), and Nicaragua (1985–87) are classified as pegs (with the dollar), despite each having undergone several devaluations, resulting in total depreciations of 10 percent, 41 percent, and 106 percent, respectively. In the case of floats, central banks can subordinate monetary policies to eliminate fluctuations in the exchange rate, rendering a de jure float equivalent to a de facto peg. India (1993–96) and Bolivia (1985–90) are examples of this pattern.

To mitigate some of these problems, I use a classification that is a combination of de jure and de facto approaches. Chart 1 shows the evolution of the number of fixed, intermediate (fixed but frequent adjusters, cooperative arrangements, floats within a predetermined range, and heavily managed floats), and flexible regimes. At first glance, the developing world seems to be marching steadily toward floating exchange-rate arrangements.

Guillermo Calvo and Carmen Reinhart suggest, however, that the so-called demise of fixed exchange rates, as evidenced by chart 1—even using a "corrected" classification—is a myth.[2] Their evidence on the unconditional volatility of exchange rates and foreign

---

2. G. Calvo and C. Reinhart, "Fear of Floating" (January 2000), *www.bsos.umd.edu/econ/ciecalvo.htm* and C. Reinhart, "The Mirage of Floating Exchange Rates," *American Economic Review* 90 (May 2000).

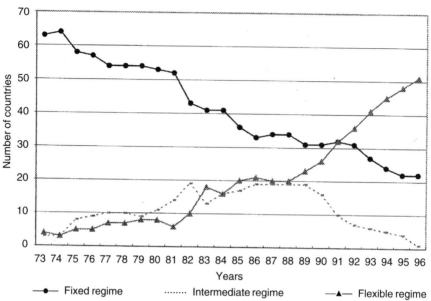

Chart 1.   Evolution of Exchange-Rate Regimes for Developing Countries
(1973–1996)

reserves suggests that many countries claiming to pursue flexible
rates are heavily intervening in the foreign exchange market to
prevent their nominal exchange rates from moving freely. Hence,
they doubt that the regimes described as flexible are substantively
different from the fixed ones. The results presented below contrast
sharply with this conclusion.

Consider two economies with different exchange-rate regimes
but otherwise possessed of the same degree of openness, financial
access, and fiscal policies. How will these economies be differen-
tially affected in terms of changes in real output and real exchange
rates when subjected to a negative terms of trade shock? The empirical evidence on this issue is contained in figures 1–4.

We see from the figures that the conventional wisdom that floating regimes are better suited to cope with terms-of-trade shocks
receives ample support. The effect of shocks to the terms of trade

on real output in the fixed exchange-rate regime is large and significant. In contrast, in regimes that can use the nominal exchange rate to buffer the shock, the effects are small. Furthermore, the response of the real exchange rate to a negative terms-of-trade shocks is markedly different across the regimes. In pegs, the real depreciation is small and occurs only two years after the shock, while in floats the real exchange rate depreciates immediately and significantly. Moreover, the shock is inflationary in floats and deflationary in pegs (not seen in the figures).

The responses of the real and nominal exchange rates are consistent with the automatic stabilizing property of regimes with flexible nominal rates and with the whole burden of the relative price adjustment relying on home (sticky) prices in fixed regimes. Results are also consistent with the relatively high costs that pegs have to pay to maintain their parity (after a 10 percent fall in the terms of trade, real output falls by 1.7 percent more in the average peg compared to the average float). The real exchange-rate response also gives empirical validity to a proposition found repeatedly in policy discussions regarding developing countries, namely, that in a small country the worsening of the terms of trade will result in a depreciation of the real exchange rate.

Finally, the magnitude of the response of the nominal exchange rate in flexible regimes (around 8 percent two years after the shock) suggests that they have no "fear of floating" when hit by this type of shock. This finding is opposite to the spirit of the results of Calvo and Reinhart. Furthermore, even when I restrict the sample to highly dollarized countries, where the Calvo-Reinhart effect should be strongest,[3] the nominal exchange rate reacts substantially in flexible regimes to terms-of-trade changes.

---

3. They argue that the fear of inflation and the existence of large sectors of the economy indebted in foreign currency or, as it has been dubbed, "liability dollarized" can prevent these countries from using exchange-rate policy.

Figure 1: Under Fixed Regime

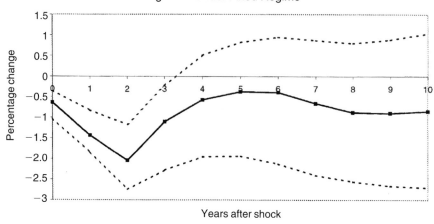

Years after shock

Figure 3: Under Flexible Regime

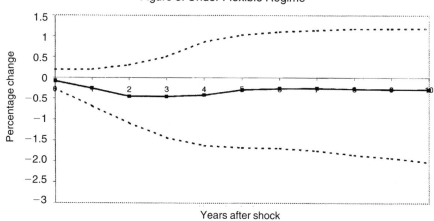

Years after shock

Figures 1–4.   Real Output Response to a 10 Percent Permanent Fall in Terms of Trade.   Notes: 1. Focusing on figure 1, in fixed regimes, real output falls by 0.6 percent in the same period the economy is hit by the negative shock. One period after the shock, real output falls an additional 0.8 percent, to a total of 1.4 percent, and so on. Solid lines are estimates of these magnitudes. Dashed lines represent 90 percent confidence-interval bounds of these estimates, that is, there is a 90 percent chance that the true estimate is within these lines. The remaining figures are to be interpreted similarly.

Figure 2: Under Fixed Regime

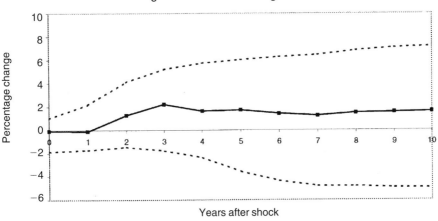

Years after shock

Figure 4: Under Flexible Regime

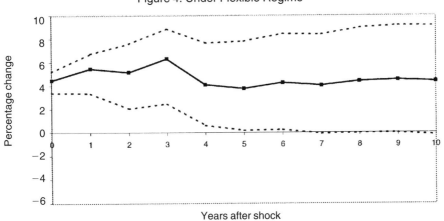

Years after shock

Figures 1–4 (*continued*). Notes (*continued*): 2. Figures interpreted as in note 1. 3. A rise in the real exchange rate implies a depreciation of the domestic currency.

Conclusions

The results presented show that, in the developing world, flexible exchange-rate regimes can better insulate the economy from real disturbances. Floats have smoother real output paths after terms-of-trade shocks. There also seems to be no fear of floating in response to terms-of-trade shocks because the floating countries typically let their nominal exchange rate depreciate considerably when hit by negative shocks. Furthermore, terms-of-trade shocks are inflationary in floats and deflationary in pegs.

The fixed-versus-flexible debate is still a highly contentious one. In the search for clearer answers, however, we ought to examine the theoretical arguments involved and quantify the relative performance of the regimes. In my research, I have found support for the conventional wisdom regarding the insulating properties of flexible regimes to real shocks. Although this benefit comes at the expense of a more volatile real exchange rate, the magnitudes involved suggest that these insulating properties are, indeed, a powerful argument in favor of flexible regimes for countries that face mostly real shocks.

Eduardo Borensztein
Jeromin Zettelmeyer

7
Monetary Independence in Emerging Markets: The Role of the Exchange-Rate Regime

How much do emerging market economies benefit from having an autonomous monetary policy? This is a question that must be considered when evaluating the pros and cons of *dollarization*, that is, of adopting a foreign currency as the legal tender of the country. A country that *dollarizes* effectively transfers all monetary policy decisions to the U.S. Federal Reserve Board. Similarly, a firm, permanent peg, such as a currency board arrangement, also implies essentially giving up the possibility of having a monetary policy (and, obviously, an exchange-rate policy). This question is of consequence because there are situations, such as responding to a negative terms-of-trade shock or trying to stim-

We thank Andy Berg for discussions that led to the conception of this paper and Xuan-Hui Ng for superb research assistance. For an extended version of this paper that contains some additional results, see Eduardo Borensztein, Jeromin Zettelmeyer and Thomas Philippon, "Monetary Independence in Emerging Markets: Does the Exchange-Rate Regime Make a Difference?" IMF Working Paper WP/01/1, January 2001. Adapted with permission of the International Monetary Fund. The views expressed in this paper are the authors' and should not be attributed to the International Monetary Fund.

ulate the domestic economy out of a recession, where the ability to affect interest rates and exchange rates may, in principle, be a valuable instrument.

In this paper we attempt to evaluate the degree of monetary independence across different exchange regimes. Defining monetary independence in a precise way is not straightforward when one considers the decisions made by a central bank in some detail. Broadly, we define monetary independence as the leeway that a central bank has to set domestic interest rates without concern for the effect on the value of the domestic currency in foreign exchange terms or the international reserves position. The United States enjoys a high level of monetary independence because the Fed manages monetary policy with a view to maintaining desirable levels of inflation and economic growth, largely neglecting the exchange rate of the U.S. dollar or the repercussions of monetary policy actions on the exchange rate of the U.S. dollar. Few, if any, other countries conduct monetary policy with a similar lack of concern about the foreign exchange market.

The question that we investigate in this paper is how economies with different exchange regimes react to changes in U.S. interest rates and in international financial market conditions. In principle, floating exchange rates provide a basis for an independent monetary policy. Under a pegged exchange-rate regime, domestic interest rates will follow closely changes in U.S. interest rates and in the international risk premium, that is, they are highly sensitive to U.S. monetary policy and international financial market developments. In contrast, economies with floating exchange rates can, in principle, accommodate international interest-rate shocks by allowing the exchange rate to adjust. The extent to which domestic interest rates actually react should depend on the monetary policy framework adopted. Under inflation targeting, for example, if an increase in U.S. interest rates causes the domestic currency to depreciate significantly, the central bank is likely to tighten monetary policy to temper the increase in inflation resulting from the pass-through of the depreciation into domestic prices. Thus, the overall effect of the increase in U.S. interest rates will be some increase in domestic interest rates and some exchange-rate depreciation, whereas in a pegged regime the effect should be felt fully by domestic interest rates.

In the turbulent international financial environment of the past few years, however, this view has been called into question. It has been argued that in the presence of external liabilities denominated in international currencies, volatility in international financial markets forces monetary policy in floating regimes into a "defensive mode" to avoid currency crises. An expansionary monetary policy, or allowing the exchange rate to depreciate significantly, would risk starting a panic among financial investors and trigger sharp capital outflows or even a currency collapse. Thus, monetary and exchange-rate policy are effectively not available as policy options, and there is no advantage to having a floating exchange rate or a national currency. In fact, because of the fear of possible negative market reactions, floating exchange-rate countries may be even more constrained than fixed-rate ones in their response to external shocks.[1]

The Tests

To investigate this question we focus on the extremes of exchange-rate regimes: currency boards and floating exchange rates. We contrast Argentina with Mexico in Latin America and Hong Kong with Singapore in Asia, that is, the countries with the longest history in

---

1. Paradoxically, it has been suggested that dollarization could break this type of link to international financial markets by changing market perceptions to such an extent that the country no longer belongs in the emerging-market risk class. The case of Panama, however, illustrates the fact that dollarization per se is not sufficient to elevate a country above the emerging-market risk class.

recent times of currency board arrangements and floating exchange-rate systems, respectively. Focusing on the polar cases has the advantage of making it more likely that we will find a sharper contrast in the implications of the exchange-rate system. Furthermore, there is a growing view that intermediate regimes are not likely to be feasible in a world of high capital mobility; the comparison of the polar exchange-rate cases may then be the only relevant one in the future. We also included a few more advanced countries with floating exchange-rate regimes: Australia, Canada, and New Zealand.

Analyzing the question at hand presents some methodological difficulties. Domestic interest rates (and the exchange rate) are affected by many variables in addition to U.S. interest rates or the international risk premium. In the context of a simple relation between domestic interest rates and U.S. rates, this will at best add noise and at worst bias the results if U.S. and domestic interest rates are both affected by common shocks. For example, an increase in oil prices may prompt the Federal Reserve Board to increase interest rates to arrest inflationary pressures; the Banco de Mexico may do the same thing, although not in response to the U.S. monetary policy change. Other shocks may cause interest rates to move in opposite directions in the two countries. This would happen, for example, as a result of a "flight to quality" by international investors. In the wake of the Russian and Long-Term Capital Management (LTCM) crises in August 1998, for example, international investors fled from emerging-market debt into safer assets such as U.S. Treasury bonds; this response alone would tend to make interest rates move in opposite directions in the United States and Mexico. Moreover, the Federal Reserve Board eased monetary policy, whereas the Banco de Mexico had to respond to a fast depreciation of the exchange rate by tightening its monetary stance. Ideally, we would like to isolate from or control for those shocks that cause an extraneous influence and focus on the impact of U.S. monetary policy shocks on emerging markets.

We follow three different approaches to examine the impact of U.S. monetary policy shocks on countries with different exchange-rate regimes. The first is an event study of monetary policy actions. The second is an econometric approach involving two or three financial variables at the daily frequency. The third is an econometric approach at the monthly frequency that includes a standard small-scale macroeconomic system.

The first approach identifies monetary policy actions taken by the United States and investigates their impact on interest rates and, where relevant, exchange rates in other countries. The monetary policy actions are identified as the days in which the Federal Open Market Committee (FOMC) of the Federal Reserve Board decided to change the federal funds target rate. These are well-identified and highly watched events by financial markets worldwide; by concentrating on changes in interest rates on dates of Fed actions one can be reasonably sure that coincidence with spurious factors is minimized; in addition, we check that the Fed actions were not themselves a response to other news hitting markets on that precise day. The problem, however, is that all monetary policy actions are, to some extent, expected. If the Fed raises interest rates when it is fully expected by financial markets, nothing will happen to financial variables in the United States and other countries. Thus, rather than taking the change in the federal funds rate itself, we use the change in short-term (three-month) Treasury Bill rates (on the day of a Fed action) as the measure of the monetary policy "shock." This change will be associated with the extent to which the action was unexpected and is thus a better measure of the information to which interest rates and exchange rates in other countries will react. An alternative measure of the impact of the monetary policy action can be obtained by comparing the level of the federal funds rate after the action with the federal funds futures rate that prevailed just before the Fed action. Both measures of the impact of monetary policy actions are in fact quite similar and generate similar results.

The disadvantage of this approach is that it provides a relatively limited number of observations.

Our second approach is to use the full time-series data of daily observations of U.S. interest rates, domestic interest rates, and, where applicable, the exchange rate in an econometric system. Although subject to the potential biases mentioned above, this procedure permits us to examine the relationship of interest for the whole available sample. The method also allows for a more general structure of lags in the relationship. One advantage in this case is that it is safe to make the assumption that U.S. interest rates are exogenous to changes in Mexican interest rates, for example, which facilitates the identification of the system. Yet there is one factor that may pollute the relationship between U.S. and domestic interest rates that was particularly strong in recent years: volatility in international financial markets. This factor can be controlled for, in principle, by adding to the system a variable measuring the international risk premium, such as the average spread on emerging-markets external debt, as measured by J.P. Morgan's Emerging Markets Bond Index (EMBI). Moreover, the reaction of domestic financial variables to the international risk premium under different exchange-rate regimes is of policy interest by itself. Therefore, to evaluate the performance of floating versus fixed exchange-rate systems, it is important also to consider their response to international risk premium changes.

Our third approach is to estimate the system at monthly intervals, incorporating the variables that are standard in small-scale macroeconomic models: the money supply, output (measured by industrial production), and inflation, in addition to the international risk premium. The advantage of the larger system is that it accounts for other factors that influence domestic interest rates, which, if excluded, may bias the relationship we are trying to isolate. The disadvantage is that working at lower frequency makes it more difficult to identify the policy effects we are investigating. It turns out that the main results are fairly robust to the three approaches adopted.

The Results

As regards the impact of U.S. monetary policy actions, the effect on Hong Kong rates is close to one for one, and even larger on Argentina's rates.[2] The impact is much lower on the floating exchange-rate countries; the estimated coefficient is less than 0.5, and it is not statistically different from 0 in various cases. The scatter diagrams in figure 1 display the relationship between the change in U.S. Treasury Bills rates (the impact of U.S. monetary policy actions) and changes in domestic interest rates in Hong Kong and Singapore on days in which the FOMC decided to change interest rates.

Perhaps surprisingly, we mostly did not detect a significant reaction of the *exchange rate* in the six countries with floats or managed floats to U.S. monetary policy actions. However, while statistically significant in only two cases, the size of the coefficients was fairly similar across countries. A 1-point increase in the U.S. Treasury Bill rate is associated with a depreciation of the domestic currency of around 1 percent in most cases.

The results from the daily frequency systems are qualitatively similar. The impact of changes in the U.S. interest rate (measured as either the ninety-day Treasury Bill rate or as unexpected changes in the federal funds rate)[3] is generally significant across the board, but the impact is higher for the currency board countries. For example, an increase of ten basis points in U.S. interest rates increases interest

---

2. The estimates are less precise in the Argentine case, where various measures of interest rates were used because the most appropriate rates (money market rates at sixty or ninety days maturity) are available only for a limited time period.

3. This is measured as the difference between the average federal funds rate and the one-month federal funds futures rate on the last day of the preceding month.

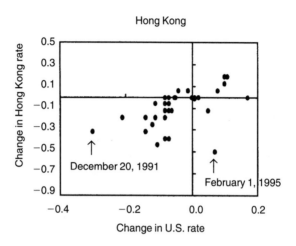

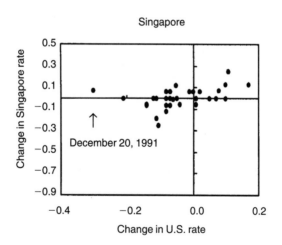

Figure 1.

rates, over a period of five days, by about ten to twelve basis points in Hong Kong and by about ten to thirty basis points in Argentina but only by about two to four basis points in Singapore; the effect in Mexico is in fact statistically insignificant due to imprecise estimation. The daily system does detect a significant effect on the exchange rate of Singapore, with a hundred-basis-point increase in U.S. interest rates causing a 0.5 percent depreciation of the Singaporean dollar. For the "control" floating-rate countries, we find an effect on interest rates in the order of 4–6 points in Australia and New Zealand and 6–8 points in Canada, and only small effects on exchange rates.

Increases in the international risk premium (measured as the average spread in emerging markets bonds) have a strong impact on domestic interest rates in Mexico and Argentina (of about the same magnitude) and in Hong Kong for the period after the Asian crisis. No such effect could be detected in Singapore, where the reaction is marginally negative, suggesting a safe-haven effect.

The systems at the monthly frequency generally indicate a stronger effect of U.S. interest rates on domestic interest rates. Again the impact is stronger in Hong Kong (between one to one and one-half to one) and Argentina (two to one or higher). There is a loss of statistical significance in the case of Singapore but higher significance in Mexico, Australia, New Zealand, and Canada. Emerging-market spreads are again significant in Latin America but not in Asia.

In summary, the following are the main findings:

- We found a significant impact of U.S. interest rates on domestic interest rates for both currency board countries and floating-rate countries. The effect, however, is significantly larger for the currency board countries Hong Kong and Argentina relative to Singapore, Australia, New Zealand, and Canada. The comparison with Mexico is hampered by imprecise estimation. This finding is fairly consistent across the three methods applied.

- Changes in EMBI spreads affect domestic financial variables significantly in both Argentina and Mexico, with roughly equal effects. However, Singapore seems to react much less to such shocks than Hong Kong.

These results are broadly consistent with the traditional view that floating exchange-rate regimes give some degree of monetary control to the central bank. The main puzzle that remains is why floating exchange rates do not seem to have been successful in shielding interest rates in Mexico from shocks to international risk premia. This is not easily attributable to "fear of floating" since exchange rates in Mexico also reacted very strongly to such shocks.

Luis Felipe Céspedes
Roberto Chang
Andrés Velasco

8
Dollarization of Liabilities, Financial Fragility, and Exchange-Rate Policy

The conduct of monetary and exchange-rate policy is perhaps the most contentious aspect of the policy response to the Asian crisis and other recent crises in emerging markets. Many analysts, led by the IMF's Stanley Fischer, have contended that stopping the exchange-rate depreciation was priority number one. Confidence, a reversal of capital flows, and growth would follow. Enthusiasts of this policy pointed to the 1995 example of Mexico (Dornbusch 1998):

> Mexico fully implemented a stark U.S.-IMF program of tight money to stabilize the currency and restore confidence. Starting in a near-meltdown situation, confidence returned and within a year the country was on the second leg of a V-shaped recovery. The IMF is unqualifiedly right in its insistence on high rates as the front end of stabilization.

Not everyone agrees. The attack on tight money was spearheaded by Joseph Stiglitz, then chief economist at the World Bank, who was not shy about making the headlines with criticisms of the sister institution. These objections went far beyond the traditional criticism of tough policies to defend a fixed exchange rate: that they are too costly in terms of output or employment. In much of East Asia the policy seemed not only to be painful, but also ineffective. *The Global Economic Prospects* published by the World Bank (1998) worried that high interest rates had little success in reducing pressure on currencies or stabilizing investor confidence, while at the same time imposing large output costs. This was the case whether the initial package entailed new agreements with the multilateral institutions (Indonesia, Korea, Thailand) or not (Malaysia and the Philippines).[1]

That the chief economist of the World Bank should disagree with his institution's own policies is peculiar. Even more peculiar was that this debate should be taking place at all. After all, monetary policies are supposed to be countercyclical: a monetary expansion is presumably called for to offset a shock to productivity or world demand. But what Dornbusch is advocating is a procyclical monetary policy, tightening in response to adverse shocks. How can this be?

Conventional theory, as exemplified by the Mundell-Fleming model, does call for countercyclical monetary policy. And in order to make such policy possible, the exchange rate should be flexible.[2] The logic behind this prescription is due to Milton Friedman (1953). If prices move slowly, it is both faster and less costly to move the

---

1. Arguably the problems resulted from policies that were "too little, too late." Corsetti, Pesenti, and Roubini (1998), in particular, have maintained that the common perception that high interest rates were the prevalent East Asian response to the crisis is a half-truth at best. The fund has insisted on the policy, but whether countries have followed it is a different matter. There is also an issue of timing. Tight money was adopted with much delay in several countries, as Corsetti, Pesenti, and Roubini (1998) show.

2. With free capital mobility and fixed exchange rates, a monetary expansion is quickly undone, as the central bank is forced to sell reserves to defend the peg. The net result is a loss of reserves with no net expansion of the monetary base.

nominal exchange rate in response to a shock that requires an adjustment in the real exchange rate. The alternative is to wait until excess demand in the goods and labor market pushes nominal goods prices down. One need not be an unreconstructed Keynesian to suspect that such a process is likely to be painful and protracted. The analogy that Friedman used is revealing, and accurate: every summer it is easier to move to daylight savings time than to coordinate large numbers of people and move all activities by an hour.

That basic policy prescription is still found in textbooks and continues to be taught to undergraduates but has come under attack recently from both academic economists and policy gurus. The real-world trigger for this shift, of course, was the Asian crisis. Countries like Indonesia that let their exchange rates go early on endured substantial real depreciations and seemed, at least at first, to be more troubled than those countries that held on. An overshooting exchange rate was blamed for debt-service difficulties, bank and corporate bankruptcies, and, in some cases, rising inflation.

The New Skeptics

The academic onslaught on countercyclical exchange rates includes the work of Calvo (1999 and 2000), Calvo and Reinhart (2000), Krugman (1999 and 2000), Stein, Hausmann, Gavin, and Pagés-Serra (1999), Hausmann, Panizza, and Stein (1999), and Aghion, Bachetta and Banerjee (2000). Details differ, but skeptical arguments about the usefulness of countercyclical monetary and exchange-rate policy are built upon the following blocks:

- *The transfer problem.*   External shocks, such as a fall in export demand, may require large real devaluations to restore the trade balance or the current account to equilibrium.

- *Dollarization of liabilities.*   If debts are denominated in dollars while firms depend on local currency revenues (or, more pre-

cisely, revenues increase with the relative price of goods pro-
duced at home), sharp and unexpected changes in relative
prices matter for financial stability.

- *Balance sheets and risk premia.*   If a sharp devaluation wreaks
  havoc with bank and corporate balance sheets, country risk
  premia will increase as foreign lenders become wary of lending
  to what seems like an increasingly risky economy.

This combination of factors is particularly prevalent in so-called
emerging markets. It can cause, the skeptics argue, the domestic
effects of external shocks to be magnified and made persistent. In
other cases it opens the door to multiple equilibria, so that the mere
expectation of a large devaluation causes one to occur; in turn, the
devaluation damages financial health enough to validate pessimistic
expectations.

But perhaps the most striking implication of the analysis is that
monetary policy becomes ineffective in offsetting real shocks. In an
open economy, an interest-rate cut operates primarily by allowing
the exchange rate to devalue so as to make local products cheaper
abroad. But if debts are dollarized, then a nominal devaluation might
increase drastically the carrying costs of the dollar debt, generating
a wave of corporate and bank bankruptcies and potentially causing
output to contract.[3]

Skeptical Thoughts on the Skeptics' Arguments

This recent line of thinking on the limitations faced by exchange-
rate and monetary policy in emerging markets is extremely useful.
It places our attention squarely where it should be: on the financial
sector and its interaction with the rest of the economy. It is primarily

---

3. This danger has been stressed in some interpretations of the Asian crisis—
particularly that of Corsetti, Pesenti, and Roubini (1998).

that sector that complicates the conduct of countercyclical policy. And, as we know from the work of Kaminsky and Reinhart (1999), financial and currency troubles increasingly tend to happen together.

But there are a number of caveats. Perhaps the most important is that, if a real depreciation is called for because of an external shock, it will take place regardless of the exchange-rate system. Policy will only determine the manner of adjustment. Under flexible rates the change in relative prices occurs suddenly and sharply. Under fixed rates or a currency board the real depreciation will take place slowly, as nominal prices fall. Throughout the adjustment period markets will anticipate the real depreciation, and hence domestic real rates will rise above world rates. And if there are doubts about the sustainability of the peg, interest rates will be even higher. At the end of the day, the real value of debt service will have risen relative to the price of haircuts. This process can conceivably wreck corporate and bank balance sheets just as surely as devaluation.

The other crucial theoretical point is that observing that debt is in dollars is not sufficient to conclude that a nominal and real depreciation will worsen the balance sheet of domestic firms. In Céspedes, Chang, and Velasco (2000) we study the point formally, using a model of a small open economy in which, as in Bernanke and Gertler (1989) and Bernanke, Gertler, and Gilchrist (1998), real exchange rates play a central role in the adjustment process, wages are sticky, liabilities are dollarized, and the country risk premium is endogenously determined by the net worth of domestic entrepreneurs. Hence all the basic building blocks are there for unexpected real exchange-rate movements to be financially dangerous and for flexible exchange rates to be destabilizing. Nonetheless, the Mundell-Fleming logic survives pretty much unscathed: flexible exchange rates do play an insulating role in the presence of real external shocks, and for some parameter values fluctuations in home output and investment are larger and more persistent under fixed than under flexible exchange rates. Such conclusions hold despite potentially large balance sheet effects.

The intuition is as follows: after an external shock, the initial devaluation of the exchange rate tends to reduce net worth since debt is denominated in dollars. This could suggest that net worth is lower in the case of floating and therefore that the country risk premium and domestic interest rates are higher and future investment lower. But that conclusion turns out to be premature. The reason is that net worth also depends on the level of current output, which flexible rates help stabilize through standard channels. The net result is that following an adverse shock net worth may well be higher under flexible than under fixed rates.

Gertler, Gilchrist, and Natalucci (2000) arrive at a similar conclusion, also using a financial accelerator model la Bernanke-Gertler. Shocks have a much greater effect on the real economy under fixed rates than under flexible rates. This is because an exchange-rate peg forces the central bank to adjust the interest rate in a manner that enhances financial distress. Such an effect occurs even if debt is denominated in units of foreign currency.

What are the implications of this work for the conduct of monetary policy in the open economy? Under a flexible exchange-rate system, should the central bank cut rates in reaction to an adverse shock? Chang and Velasco (2000a) argue that in most circumstances they should, even if there is dollar debt, because a devaluation has at least two other, more conventional expansionary effects: it lowers domestic interest rates and it causes expenditures to switch toward domestic goods.

Aghion, Bachetta, and Banerjee (2000) and Christiano, Gust, and Roldós (2000) consider the same questions using models that stress the role of collateral in allowing domestic firms to borrow abroad. In this case, a nominal and real devaluation can lower the dollar value of such collateral, causing foreign lending and therefore domestic investment and growth to fall. Again, the key policy question is, Should the home economy respond with an interest rate cut or a hike? The answer is, *it all depends*. In Aghion, Bachetta, and Banerjee (2000), an interest rate cut is called for if the share of dollar debt is sufficiently small, and if the competitiveness effect of devaluation is strong enough. In Christiano, Gust, and Roldós (2000), if there are substantial substitution possibilities among factors of production, and diminishing returns are not too great, then an interest rate cut will produce an expansion; otherwise, it will produce a contraction.

Our discussion yields at least two lessons. First, the recent emphasis on the relationship between exchange rates and financial variables is here to stay and, as argued at length in Chang and Velasco (2000b), has important implications for exchange rate theory and policy. Second, it is at least too early to conclude that, because of dollarization of liabilities and financial imperfections, policymakers should give up on the hope of carrying out countercyclical monetary and exchange-rate policies. There are circumstances in which those policies will work as conventional theory predicts. And of course, policymakers can also endeavor to correct distortions that pose limitations for macropolicy: with stronger local banks, deeper markets for domestic currency debt, and more independent monetary authorities, there will be even more scope for cushioning the shocks that inevitably hit economies.

References

Aghion, P., P. Bacchetta, and A. Banerjee. "Currency Crises in an Economy with Credit Constraints." Unpublished manuscript, MIT and Lausanne, June 2000.

Bernanke, B., and M. Gertler. "Agency Costs, Net Worth, and Business Fluctuations." *American Economic Review* 79 (1989): 14–31.

Bernanke, B., M. Gertler, and S. Gilchrist. "The Financial Accelerator in a Quantitative Business Cycle Framework." NBER Working Paper 6455, March 1998.

Calvo, G. "Fixed vs. Flexible Exchange Rates: Preliminaries of a Turn-of-Millennium Rematch." May 1999. At http://www.bsos.umd.edu/econ/.

Calvo, G. "Capital Market and the Exchange Rate with Special Reference to the Dollarization Debate in Latin America." April 2000. At http://www.bsos.umd.edu/econ/.

Calvo, G., and C. Reinhart. "Fear of Floating." Paper presented to the Conference on Currency Unions, Hoover Institution, Stanford University, May 2000.

Céspedes, L. F., R. Chang, and A. Velasco. "Balance Sheets and Exchange Rates." NBER Working Paper No. 7840, August 2000.

Chang, R., and A. Velasco. "Dollarization of Liabilities, Balance Sheet Vulnerability and Monetary Policy." Manuscript, Harvard University, May 2000a.

Chang, R., and A. Velasco. "Exchange Rate Regimes for Developing Countries." *American Economic Review* 90 (2) (2000b): 71–75.

Christiano, L., C. Gust, and J. Roldós. "Monetary Policy in a Financial Crisis." Manuscript, Northwestern University, November 2000.

Corsetti, G., P. Pesenti, and N. Roubini. "What Caused the Asian Currency and Financial Crises? Part I: Macroeconomic Overview." NBER Working Paper 6833, December 1998.

Dornbusch, R. "After Asia: New Directions for the International Financial System." At http://web.mit.edu/rudi/www/.

Eichengreen, B., and R. Hausmann. "Financial Fragility and Exchange Rates." Paper presented at the Annual Conference of the Federal Reserve Bank of Kansas City, Jackson Hole, Wyoming, August 1999.

Friedman, Milton. *Essays in Positive Economics.* Chicago: University of Chicago Press, 1953.

Galí, J., and T. Monacelli. "Optimal Monetary Policy and Exchange Rate Volatility in a Small Open Economy." November 1999.

Gertler, M., S. Gilchrist, and F. M. Natalucci. "External Constraints on Monetary Policy and the Financial Accelerator." Manuscript, New York University, 2000.

Global Economic Prospects and the Developing Countries. Washington, D.C.: World Bank, 1998.

Hausmann, R., U. Panizza, and E. Stein. "Why Do Countries Float the Way

They Float?" Working Paper No. 418, Inter-American Development Bank, 1999.

Hellman, T., K. Murdoch, and J. E. Stiglitz. "Addressing Moral Hazard in Banking: Deposit Rate Controls vs. Capital Requirements." Unpublished manuscript, 1994.

Kaminsky, Graciela L., and Carmen M. Reinhart. "The Twin Crises: The Causes of Banking and Balance-of-Payments Problems." *American Economic Review* 89 (3) (June 1999): 473–500.

Krugman, P. "Balance Sheets, the Transfer Problem and Financial Crises." In *International Finance and Financial Crises*, ed. P. Isard, A. Razin, and A. Rose. Kluwer Academic Publishers, 1999.

Krugman, P. "Analytical Afterthoughts on the Asian Crisis." At http://web.mit.edu/krugman/www/MINICRIS.htm.

Krugman, P., and L. Taylor. "Contractionary Effects of Devaluation." *Journal of International Economics* 8 (August 1978): 445–56.

Lizondo, J. S., and P. Montiel. "Contractionary Devaluation in Developing Countries: An Analytical Overview." IMF Staff Papers 36, March 1989, pp. 182–227.

Obstfeld, M., and K. Rogoff. "Exchange Rate Dynamics Redux." *Journal of Political Economy* 103 (1995): 624–60.

Obstfeld, M., and K. Rogoff. "New Directions for Stochastic Open Economy Models." *Journal of International Economics* 50 (2000): 117–54.

Stein, E. H., R. Hausmann, Michael Gavin, and C. Pagés-Serra. "Financial Turmoil and Choice of Exchange Rate Regime." Working Paper, Research Department, IADB, January 1999. Also at http://www.iadb.org/oce.

Maurice Obstfeld
Kenneth Rogoff

9
Do We Really Need a New Global Monetary Compact?

Over the past fifteen years, there has emerged a widespread consensus that monetary policy should be delegated to an independent central bank, one that primarily focuses on inflation but also pays attention to the general health of the economy. Literally dozens of countries have engaged in dramatic institutional reform—often involving constitutional amendments—so as to greatly increase the level of independence of their central banks. Converts include England, Canada, the euro zone, and many developing countries. These changes have almost certainly been a major factor in the return to low inflation we have witnessed throughout much of the world over the past decade and a half. True, there remains quite a bit of controversy about the details. Is it better to rely on having a conservative central bank board, or is it preferable to try to have the government legislate incentive contracts? How much accountability should the central bank have to the main legislature? How much transparency is needed? But today, credibility increasingly takes a backseat to implementation in central bank debate, hence the large and growing literature on "optimal (John)

Taylor rules" for setting interest rates in response to inflation and output data.

Curiously, as new central bank constitutions have become increasingly set in stone, little attention has been paid to international spillover effects. Is it a problem that the United States pays so little attention to Europe's interests in designing its rule and vice versa? Certainly, smaller countries such as Canada, though important as a group, pay absolutely no attention to spillover effects to the United States and elsewhere. Should we be rethinking the whole process of central bank reform to ensure that international spillovers are given more attention? The recent plight of the euro, which has fallen by more than 25 percent against the dollar since its inception, is a case in point, as is Japan's severe recession. For example, it would be far easier for Japan to use loose monetary policy to counter its severe recession if the United States and Europe shared the burden of the global expansion, thereby alleviating pressure for (perhaps) excessive devaluation of the yen. One of the main lessons of the academic literature on international monetary cooperation from the 1970s and 1980s is that, in certain circumstances, international monetary policy coordination failures can be quite dramatic.

In their paper in this volume, Obstfeld and Rogoff make a first attempt at tackling this kind of issue. The answer they get, in brief, is that the current trend in central bank design, which pays very little attention to global spillovers, might not be so bad. Under what seem to be rather reasonable assumptions, they find that the gain to coordinating international efforts at central bank reform are likely to be very small. Indeed, halfway efforts at coordination (such as Ronald McKinnon's world money standard or John Williamson's target zones for exchange rates) might well prove inferior to the outcome we have now, where coordination of rule setting is quite limited. Thus, for example, if countries each unilaterally implement domestically optimal Taylor rules while using institutional reform to overcome inflation credibility problems, then the result may be nearly as good as under a global monetary authority. And, of course, any costs of negotiating and policing international agreements are avoided. It is only when countries adopt really bad policies—policies that are bad even in terms of pure self-interest—that spillovers start to really matter. (Thus, if it is true that Japan is running a very poorly designed monetary policy rule, as many have argued, then the United States and Europe should indeed care.)

In Obstfeld and Rogoff's model, domestic monetary policy essentially operates through four channels, each corresponding to a different distortion in the economy. One channel is sticky wages, without which monetary policy would be neutral. This is the usual effect present in earlier models. But there are other important effects as well. One is through international risk sharing, which can be substantially affected by the international monetary system. Thus, if international markets are not complete, the way in which Europe and the United States share the burden of international monetary stabilization policy matters. The idea of international risk sharing may seem rather obscure in terms of conventional discussions of monetary policy, but it is not. The issue of whether the United States today should intervene to support the euro is very much related to how much the United States should take into account the fact that Europe is growing at a much slower rate than the United States— that is, the lack of synchronization in business cycles.

Another channel is the terms of trade, assuming countries do not impose optimal unilateral tariffs. Again, it may seem odd to think of monetary policy as providing a substitute for tariff policy, but with a bit of further thought we can see that it is not. The monetary policy rule matters through its effects on general wage levels at home and abroad. In a world where agents care about risk, the relative levels at which wages are preset will depend on the relative risks agents are forced to bear at home and abroad. If, for example, global monetary policy is tuned so that the home exchange rate is strong when world demand is high, home agents will bear less production risk than foreign agents. Why? Because when global demand is high, the value of extra income is low, so home agents are glad to see an appreciated exchange rate that shifts world demand toward foreigners, leaving home agents more leisure time. But the relative distribution of risk then feeds back into wage levels: if foreign agents are forced to bear more exchange-rate risk, they respond by raising preset wages. This generally has the effect of reducing foreign supply, with effects on world relative prices that are much like those of a tariff.

Finally, if the economy is characterized by a high degree of monopoly, monetary policy can affect the level of that distortion. Even in a rule-based system, where the monetary authorities cannot even try to systematically fool workers, the monetary policy rule can affect the average level of real wages, again through its effects on risk.

In general, understanding policy in an environment with four distortions (sticky prices, monopoly, optimal tariff considerations, risk-sharing problems) can be very difficult since the distortions can interact. Thus, for example, one cannot simply assume that the best monetary policy from a global standpoint is one that mimics a world of flexible wages. This is simply another case where eliminating one distortion entirely is not necessarily optimal unless all distortions are removed.

With so many effects to take into account, why does it turn out that a noncooperative monetary policy gives a similar outcome to a cooperative one? That is, why is it enough for countries to clean up their own house in designing anti-inflation monetary institutions, and why aren't international spillover effects more important?

The basic point is that once a central bank is forced to adopt a rule, it faces a trade-off between balancing different distortions. For example, starting from the cooperative rule, either central bank could alter its rule to improve its country's terms of trade but only at the cost of creating an unfavorable relation between world output and the exchange rate.

The one major potential area for unambiguous gain is in risk sharing, if financial markets are incomplete. Obstfeld and Rogoff are able to characterize the policy that would be optimal from a global perspective, and they contrast this policy with the one chosen in a noncooperative setting. Using numerical methods, they find that the gain to cooperation is not quantitatively large. Indeed, it is generally at least two orders of magnitude (a factor of 100) less than the gain registered by adopting the best noncooperative monetary policies, rather than having fully flexible exchange rates with fixed money-supply paths.

The authors do not presume that theirs will necessarily be the last word on the topic of international monetary cooperation. However, their analysis should give pause to the many economists who presume that the current monetary system is vastly suboptimal and must someday give way to something like a world euro standard.

Index